Essential SQA Exam Practice

Higher MATHEMATICS

Practice Questions & Exam Papers

Questions & Papers

▶ Practise **60+ questions** covering every question type and topic

▶ Complete **2 practice papers** that mirror the real SQA exams

Robert Barclay

HODDER GIBSON
AN HACHETTE UK COMPANY

Orders: please contact Hachette UK Distribution, Hely Hutchinson Centre, Milton Road, Didcot, Oxfordshire, OX11 7HH.
Telephone: +44 (0)1235 827827. Email: education@hachette.co.uk Lines are open from 9 a.m. to 5 p.m., Monday to Friday. You can also order through our website: www.hoddereducation.co.uk. If you have queries or questions that aren't about an order, you can contact us at hoddergibson@hodder.co.uk

© Robert Barclay 2019

First published in 2019 by
Hodder Gibson, an imprint of Hodder Education
An Hachette UK Company
50 Frederick Street
Edinburgh, EH2 1EX

Impression number   5   4   3
Year   2023

Illustrations by Aptara Inc.

Typeset in Aptara Inc.

Printed and bound by CPI Group (UK) Ltd, Croydon CR0 4YY

A catalogue record for this title is available from the British Library.

ISBN: 978 1 5104 7181 8

CONTENTS

INTRODUCTION

Higher Mathematics

This book provides you with material for targeted practice so that you can revise confidently for your SQA Higher Mathematics examination. It can be used throughout the year, in key revision periods and in the lead-up to the examination.

Structure of the book

The questions in the book are split into two main sections. The first section contains groups of Practice Questions arranged by topic. The second section contains two full Practice Papers. This structure provides you with the opportunity to focus your revision on individual topics as well as completing full practice assessments.

The book also contains

▶ the Formulae list provided for the SQA Higher Mathematics examination

▶ an Answers section containing fully worked answers and marking instructions for both Practice Questions and Practice Papers

▶ Key Area index grids for the Practice Questions and Practice Papers.

The questions in both sections provide comprehensive coverage of the course content and are similar to the type of questions that will appear in the final examination, in line with the 2019 course assessment. The Practice Papers mirror the format of the final examination.

Features in the book

The Practice Questions section features:

▶ hints on how to tackle many of the questions

▶ an icon 🖩 indicating which questions require the use of a calculator. Questions which do not have this icon attached to them should be done without the use of a calculator.

The Answers section features:

▶ the 'Grade demand' of each question (C = level C; > C = above level C)

▶ commentary, hints and tips on all of the questions in the Practice Papers.

SQA Higher Mathematics examination

	Paper 1 (non-calculator)	Paper 2
Time	1 hour 15 minutes	1 hour 30 minutes
Marks	55	65
Proportion of level C questions	Approximately 65% of the marks are available for level C responses.	
Balance of skills	Approximately 65% of the marks are available for questions assessing only operational skills.	
	Approximately 35% of the marks are available for questions assessing both operational and reasoning skills.	

In the exam, you will be given separate question and answer booklets. The question booklet gives the Formulae list and all the questions, showing the number of marks allocated to each question. The answer booklet provides space for you to write your working and answers.

The question papers contain a mixture of short answer and extended response questions.

The range of notional scores for each grade in the examination is shown in the table.

Grade	A	B	C	D
Notional scores	70–100%	60–69%	50–59%	40–49%

Further details can be found in the Higher Mathematics section on the SQA website: www.sqa.org.uk/sqa/47910.html.

Some tips for achieving a good mark

Build your confidence

It is important that you go into the examination with confidence. The key to success is preparation. In order to build your confidence, work hard throughout the year to consolidate your strengths while trying to work on areas where there is room for improvement.

The students who work hardest are those who usually perform best in the examination. So the key to success is to practise, practise, practise!

Doing maths questions is the most effective use of your study time. You will benefit much more from spending 30 minutes doing maths questions than spending several hours copying out notes or reading a maths textbook.

Practise doing the type of questions that are likely to appear in the exam. Work through the Practice Questions and Practice Papers in this book, and use past SQA Higher Mathematics papers. Use the marking instructions to check your answers and to understand what the examiners are looking for. Ask your teacher for help if you get stuck.

Basic skills

You must practise essential basic skills for Higher Mathematics, such as numerical calculations, manipulating algebraic expressions, expanding brackets, solving equations and working with exact values in trigonometric expressions and equations.

Topics introduced at National 5

You must be proficient in the basic skills in topics which are introduced at National 5 (for example, vectors, indices, completing the square and problems involving straight lines) before developing more advanced skills in them during the Higher course.

Non-routine problems

It is important to practise non-routine problems, particularly in unfamiliar contexts, as often as possible throughout the course, particularly if you are aiming for an A or B pass in Higher Mathematics.

Graph sketching

Graph sketching is an important and integral part of mathematics. Practise sketching graphs on plain paper whenever possible throughout this course. Squared paper and graph paper are not allowed in the Higher Mathematics examination.

Show all working clearly

The instructions on the front of the exam paper state that 'Full credit will be given only to solutions which contain appropriate working'. A 'correct' answer with no working may only be awarded partial marks or even no marks at all. An incomplete answer will be awarded marks for any appropriate working.

Attempt every question, even if you are not sure whether you are correct. Your solution may contain working which will gain some marks. A blank response is certain to be awarded no marks. Never score out working unless you have something better to replace it with.

Make drawings

Making a rough sketch of the diagram in your answer booklet may help you interpret the question and achieve more marks. Try drawing what you visualise as the 'picture', described in each relevant question. This is a mathematical skill expected of most candidates at Higher level.

Extended response questions

You should look for connections between parts of questions, particularly where there are three or four sections to a question. These are almost always linked and, in some instances, an earlier result in part a) or b) is needed, and using it will avoid further repeated work.

Notation

Make sure that you use the correct notation. In particular, for integration questions, remember to include '*dx*' within your integral.

Radians

Remember to work in radians when attempting any question involving both trigonometry and calculus.

Simplify

Get into the habit of simplifying expressions before doing any further work with them. This should make all subsequent work easier. Be aware that numerical values in final answers must be simplified as far as possible.

Revision

You can download a Revision Calendar to use as part of your studies from our website at www.hoddergibson.co.uk/ESEP-extras

Good luck!

Remember that the rewards for passing Higher Mathematics are well worth it! Your pass will help you get the future you want for yourself. In the examination, be confident in your own ability. If you're not sure how to answer a question trust your instincts and just give it a go anyway – keep calm and don't panic!

FORMULAE LIST

Circle

The equation $x^2 + y^2 + 2gx + 2fy + c = 0$ represents a circle centre $(-g, -f)$ and radius $\sqrt{g^2 + f^2 - c}$.

The equation $(x - a)^2 + (y - b)^2 = r^2$ represents a circle centre (a, b) and radius r.

Scalar product

$\mathbf{a}.\mathbf{b} = |\mathbf{a}||\mathbf{b}|\cos\theta$, where θ is the angle between $\mathbf{a}$ and $\mathbf{b}$

or

$\mathbf{a}.\mathbf{b} = a_1b_1 + a_2b_2 + a_3b_3$, where $\mathbf{a} = \begin{pmatrix} a_1 \\ a_2 \\ a_3 \end{pmatrix}$ and $\mathbf{b} = \begin{pmatrix} b_1 \\ b_2 \\ b_3 \end{pmatrix}$.

Trigonometric formulae

$$\sin(A \pm B) = \sin A \cos B \pm \cos A \sin B$$
$$\cos(A \pm B) = \cos A \cos B \mp \sin A \sin B$$
$$\sin 2A = 2 \sin A \cos A$$
$$\cos 2A = \cos^2 A - \sin^2 A$$
$$= 2 \cos^2 A - 1$$
$$= 1 - 2 \sin^2 A$$

Table of standard derivatives

$f(x)$	$f'(x)$
$\sin ax$	$a \cos ax$
$\cos ax$	$-a \sin ax$

Table of standard integrals

$f(x)$	$\int f(x)\,dx$
$\sin ax$	$-\dfrac{1}{a}\cos ax + c$
$\cos ax$	$\dfrac{1}{a}\sin ax + c$

KEY AREA INDEX GRIDS

Practice Questions

Topic	Practice Questions
Algebraic and trigonometric skills	
▸ Functions and graphs	1–9
▸ Quadratics	10–13
▸ Polynomials	14–16
▸ Logarithms and exponentials	17–22
▸ Trigonometric formulae	23–27
▸ The wave function	28–29
Geometric skills	
▸ Vectors	30–35
Calculus skills	
▸ Differentiation	36–39
▸ Applications of differentiation	40–44
▸ Integration	45–47
▸ Applications of integration	48–51
Algebraic and geometric skills	
▸ Recurrence relations	52–55
▸ The straight line	56–58
▸ The circle	59–62

Practice Papers

Topic	Practice Paper A Paper 1	Practice Paper A Paper 2	Practice Paper B Paper 1	Practice Paper B Paper 2
Algebraic and trigonometric skills				
▸ Functions and graphs	3, 8, 10		2, 4, 8	1
▸ Quadratics	6	2		9
▸ Polynomials	11		13	
▸ Logarithms and exponentials	10	9	7	8, 11
▸ Trigonometric formulae	14	12(a)	9, 11	13
▸ The wave function		10	14	
Geometric skills				
▸ Vectors	7, 13	4,7	10	2, 4
Calculus skills				
▸ Differentiation	5		5	
▸ Applications of differentiation	9, 15	3	1	10, 12(a)
▸ Integration	12	12(b)	6	
▸ Applications of integration		6, 11	12	7, 12(b)
Algebraic and geometric skills				
▸ Recurrence relations	2			6
▸ The straight line	4	1	3	5(a)(b)
▸ The circle	1	5, 7		3, 5(c)

MARKS

Algebraic and trigonometric skills

1 A function f is given by $f(x) = \dfrac{1}{5-x}$.

   a) What value of x cannot be in the domain of f?   **1**

   b) Find $f^{-1}(x)$.   **3**

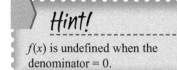

Hint!

$f(x)$ is undefined when the denominator $= 0$.

2 A function h is given by $h(x) = \sqrt{4 - x^2}$.   **2**

   Write down a suitable domain of h.

3 Functions $f(x) = 4x$ and $g(x) = 3\sin x$ are defined on suitable domains.

   a) Evaluate $f\left(g\left(\dfrac{\pi}{6}\right)\right)$.   **1**

   b) Find an expression for $g(f(x))$.   **2**

4 Functions $f(x) = \dfrac{1}{2}x - \dfrac{3}{4}$ and $g(x) = 2x + \dfrac{3}{2}$ are defined on suitable domains.

Hint!

$f(f^{-1}(x)) = x$

   a) Find an expression for $f(g(x))$.   **1**

   b) What is the connection between the functions f and g?   **2**

Hint!

This table shows the transformations associated with different functions.

Function	Transformation
$-f(x)$	Reflect in the x-axis
$f(-x)$	Reflect in the y-axis
$f(x) + a$	Vertical translation a units up
$f(x + a)$	Horizontal translation a units left
$kf(x)$	Vertical stretch by factor k
$f(kx)$	Horizontal compression by factor k
$f^{-1}(x)$	Reflect in $y = x$
$f'(x)$	Stationary points of $f(x)$ are roots of $f'(x)$

5 The diagram shows the graph of a function $y = f(x)$.

On separate diagrams sketch the graphs of:

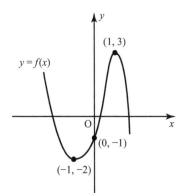

   a) $y = 3 - f(x)$;   **2**

   b) $y = 2f(x) - 1$;   **2**

   c) $y = f'(x)$.   **3**

6 The diagram shows the graph of a function $y = g(x)$.

On separate diagrams sketch the graphs of:

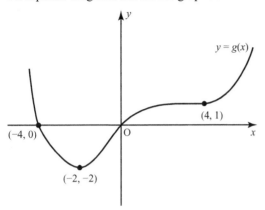

a) $y = g(2x) + 2$; **2**

b) $y = g'(x)$. **3**

7 The diagram shows part of the graph of a function whose equation is of **3**
the form $y = p\cos(x+q)° + r$.

Write down the values of p, q and r:

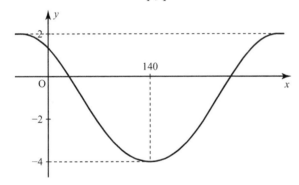

8 The function $f(x) = \log_b(x + a)$ is defined on a suitable domain.

The graph with equation $y = f(x)$ is shown in the diagram.

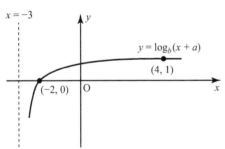

a) Find the values of a and b. **3**

b) State the domain for $f(x)$. **1**

c) Sketch the graph with equation $y = f^{-1}(x)$. **2**

9 The diagram shows the graph with equation $y = f(x)$, where $f(x) = k(x - a)(x - b)$, $a < b$.

Find the values of a, b and k.

2

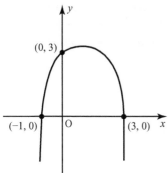

Hint!

If $x = a$ is a root then $(x - a)$ is a factor.

10 a) Express $3x^2 - 12x + 5$ in the form $a(x + b)^2 + c$.

b) Hence, state the range of values of the function $f(x) = 3x^2 - 12x + 5$.

3

1

Hint!

Complete the square for $3(x^2 - 4x)$ first, then add the 5 at the end.

11 Solve $2x^2 + 5x - 12 \leq 0$, where x is a real number.

2

Hint!

Find the roots of $2x^2 + 5x - 12 = 0$ then use a table of values or sketch a graph to find the range of values of x for which $2x^2 + 5x - 12 \leq 0$.

12 Find the range of values of k such that the equation $2x^2 + kx - k = 0$ has no real roots.

4

13 a) Find the value of k for which the line with equation $y = k$ is a tangent to the parabola with equation $y = kx^2 + 3x + 3$.

5

b) Show that the line with equation $y = k$ will touch or intersect the parabola with equation $y = kx^2 + 3x + 3$ for all real values of k.

2

14 a) Show that $x = 3$ is a root of the equation $2x^4 - x^3 - 14x^2 - 5x + 6 = 0$.

3

b) Find the other roots of the equation.

3

Hint!

$x = 3$ is a root $\Leftrightarrow (x - 3)$ is a factor.

15 When $f(x) = x^3 + px^2 + qx - 12$ is divided by $(x - 2)$, the remainder is 10.

One factor of $f(x)$ is $(x - 1)$.

Find the values of p and q.

4

Hint!

Use synthetic division to obtain a pair of simultaneous equations.

MARKS

16 a) Show that the curves with equations $y = x^3 - 12x + 1$ and $y = 5x^2 - 15x - 8$ intersect at the point where $x = -1$.

3

Hint!

Set the equations of the curves equal to each other, rearrange into standard form and solve.

b) Find the coordinates of all the points of intersection of the two curves.

4

Hints!

In questions 17–22:

➔ Conversion from logarithmic to exponential form and vice versa is required.
$\log_a x = y \Leftrightarrow x = a^y$

➔ The laws of logarithms require to be applied.

1 $\log_a x + \log_a y = \log_a xy$

2 $\log_a x - \log_a y = \log_a \dfrac{x}{y}$

3 $n \log_a x = \log_a x^n$

17 Find the value of $\dfrac{1}{2}\log_6 16 + \log_6 9$.

3

18 Given that $3\log_a 10 - \log_a 500 = \dfrac{1}{3}$, find the value of a.

4

19 Solve $\log_2(x - 6) + \log_2(x + 1) = 3$, where $x > 6$.

4

 20 A liquid cools according to the law $T_t = T_0 e^{-kt}$, where T_0 is the initial temperature and T_t is the temperature after t minutes.

All temperatures are in degrees Celsius.

A bowl of this liquid cooled from $100\,°C$ to $80\,°C$ in 10 minutes.

Hint!

Substitute the known value(s) into the equation and then evaluate the formula or solve the resulting equation.

a) Calculate the value of k.

3

b) By how many degrees will the temperature of this liquid fall in the next half an hour?

2

21 Two variables, x and y, are related by the equation $y = kx^n$.

5

If $\log_3 y$ is plotted against $\log_3 x$ the following graph is obtained.

Find the values of k and n.

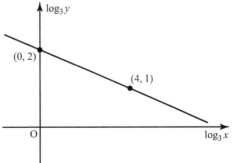

Hint!

Start by taking logarithms of both sides of $y = kx^n$ then use laws of logarithms to convert into the equation, $\log_3 y = m\log_3 x + c$, of the given straight line.

MARKS

22 Two variables, x and y, are related by the equation $y = ab^x$.

If $\log_4 y$ is plotted against x the following graph is obtained.

Find the values of a and b.

5

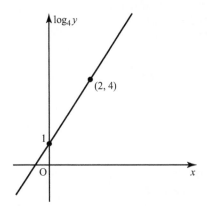

> **Hint!**
>
> In questions 23, 24 and 26–29 you will be required to use trigonometric addition or double angle formulae. These are given in the Formulae list on page vi.

23 On the coordinate diagram shown, A is the point (5, 12) and B is the point (8, 6).

Angle AOC = p and angle BOD = q.

Find the exact value of $\sin$ AOB in its simplest form.

5

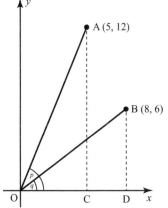

> **Hint!**
>
> Use the formula for $\sin(a - b)$ then use SOHCAHTOA in each right-angled triangle to find $\sin a$, $\sin b$, $\cos a$ and $\cos b$.

24 If $\tan x = \dfrac{1}{\sqrt{7}}$, $0 < x < \dfrac{\pi}{2}$, find the exact values of $\sin 2x$ and $\cos 2x$.

5

> **Hint!**
>
> Sketch a right-angled triangle in which $\tan x = \dfrac{1}{\sqrt{7}}$.

25 Solve $2\cos 3x° + 1 = 0$ for $0 \le x < 180$.

> *Hint!*
> If x in the range $0 \le x < 180$ then $3x$ in the range $0 \le 3x < 540$.

3

26 Solve $\cos 2\theta + \sin \theta = 0$ for $0 \le \theta < 2\pi$.

> *Hint!*
> Use an appropriate double angle formula then factorise.

5

27 Show that $\dfrac{\sin 2x}{1 + \cos 2x} = \tan x$, where $0 < x < \dfrac{\pi}{2}$.

> *Hint!*
> Use appropriate double angle formulae then simplify.

3

28 **a)** Express $4\cos x° + \sin x°$ in the form $k\cos(x - a)°$, where $k > 0$ and $0 \le a < 360$.

4

     b) Hence, solve the equation $4\cos x° + \sin x° + \sqrt{13} = 0$ for $0 \le x < 360$.

> *Hint!*
> Use the answer to part **a)** to rewrite the equation in a form that is easier to solve.

3

29 **a)** Express $\sqrt{3}\sin x - \cos x$ in the form $k\sin(x - a)$ where $k > 0$ and $0 \le a < 2\pi$.

4

     b) Hence, or otherwise, sketch the graph with equation $y = \sqrt{3}\sin x - \cos x$, $0 \le x < 2\pi$.

> *Hint!*
> Use the answer to part **a)** to rewrite the equation in terms of $\sin x$ only, then sketch the curve with this equation.

3

MARKS

Geometric skills

30 P is the point $(2, -9, 6)$, Q is $(6, -3, 4)$ and R is $(12, 6, 1)$.
Show that P, Q and R are collinear and determine the ratio in which Q divides PR.

4

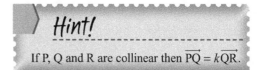

Hint!
If P, Q and R are collinear then $\overrightarrow{PQ} = k\overrightarrow{QR}$.

31 The point B divides the line joining $A(-1, -7, 8)$ to $C(5, 2, -1)$ in the ratio $2:1$.
Find the coordinates of B.

2

32 ABCD, EFGH is a cuboid.
M is the midpoint of HG.
N lies one third of the way along FG.
$\overrightarrow{AB}$, $\overrightarrow{AD}$ and $\overrightarrow{AE}$ are represented by the vectors

$$\begin{pmatrix} 2 \\ 4 \\ 0 \end{pmatrix}, \begin{pmatrix} -6 \\ 3 \\ 3 \end{pmatrix} \text{ and } \begin{pmatrix} 2 \\ -1 \\ 5 \end{pmatrix} \text{ respectively.}$$

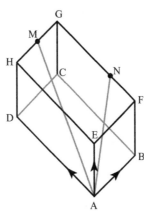

a) Calculate the components of $\overrightarrow{AM}$.

2

b) Calculate the components of $\overrightarrow{AN}$.

2

c) Calculate the size of angle MAN.

5

Hints!
a) and b) Vectors with the same direction and magnitude are equal, e.g.
$$\overrightarrow{AB} = \overrightarrow{DC}.$$

c) Use $\cos MAN = \dfrac{\overrightarrow{AM}.\overrightarrow{AN}}{\left|\overrightarrow{AM}\right|\left|\overrightarrow{AN}\right|}.$

33 Vectors **u** and **v** are defined by $\mathbf{u} = 2\mathbf{i} + 6\mathbf{k}$ and $\mathbf{v} = 3\mathbf{i} + 4\mathbf{j} - \mathbf{k}$.
Determine whether or not **u** and **v** are perpendicular to each other.

2

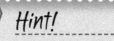

Hint!
$\mathbf{u}, \mathbf{v}$ perpendicular $\Leftrightarrow \mathbf{u}.\mathbf{v} = 0$

34 Vector **a** is such that $\mathbf{a} = 8\mathbf{i} - \sqrt{5}\mathbf{j} + 2\sqrt{3}\mathbf{k}$.
Find the value of k for which $k\mathbf{a}$ is a unit vector.

3

Hint!
Find the vector with magnitude 1 which is parallel to **a**.

35 In a square-based pyramid, all the eight edges are of length 5 units. Evaluate $\mathbf{p}.(\mathbf{q} + \mathbf{r})$.

3

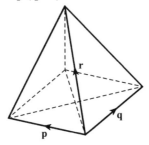

MARKS

Calculus skills

Hint!

36 Given that $y = 2\sqrt{x}(x-1) + 3\cos 2x$, find $\dfrac{dy}{dx}$.

Multiply out the brackets before differentiating.

The derivatives of $f(x) = \sin ax$ and $f(x) = \cos ax$ are given in the Formulae list.

5

Hint!

Use the chain rule for the questions 37, 38 and 39.

37 Find the rate of change of the function $f(x) = (3 - x^2)^4$ when $x = 2$.   **3**

38 Given that $P = \dfrac{3}{1-4n}$, find $\dfrac{dP}{dn}$.   **3**

39 Given that $f(x) = \sin(2x + \pi) - \cos^3 x$, find $f'(x)$.   **4**

40 A function f is given by $f(x) = \dfrac{2}{3}x^3 + 3x^2 - 8x + 1$.

Hints!

  a) Find the equation of the tangent to the curve $y = f(x)$ at the point where $x = -3$.   **4**

a) The gradient of the tangent to the curve $y = f(x)$ at the point $(a, f(a))$ is the value of $f'(a)$.

  b) Find algebraically the values of x for which the function $f(x)$ is strictly decreasing.   **3**

b) The curve with equation $y = f(x)$ is decreasing when $f'(x) < 0$.

41 A function f is defined by the formula $f(x) = (x-2)^2(x-5)$.

  a) Find the coordinates of the points where the graph of $y = f(x)$ meets the x- and y-axes.   **2**

Hint!

  b) Find the coordinates of the stationary points of the function and determine their nature.   **7**

Stationary points occur when $\dfrac{dy}{dx} = 0$.

  c) Sketch the graph of $y = f(x)$.   **1**

42 A function f is defined on the domain $-2 \le x \le 2$ by $f(x) = x^3 - 2x^2 - 7x + 1$.   **7**

Determine the maximum and minimum values of f.

Hint!

Within a closed interval the maximum and minimum values of a function are either at stationary points or at the end points of the interval.

MARKS

43 A cuboid measures x metres by $4x$ metres by h metres and its volume is 800 cubic metres.

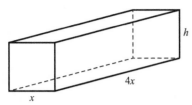

   a)   Show that the surface area, A square metres, of the cuboid is given by   **3**
$$A(x) = 8x^2 + \frac{2000}{x}.$$

   b)   Find the value of x that minimises the surface area of the cuboid.   **5**

44 A particle moves in a straight line such that its displacement, s metres, after   **6**

t seconds is given by $s = (6t+1)^{\frac{3}{2}}$.

Find its displacement, velocity and acceleration after 4 seconds.

> **Hint!**
> -
>
> Velocity, v, is the rate of change of displacement with respect to time, t, i.e. $v = \dfrac{ds}{dt}$.
>
> Acceleration, a, is the rate of change of velocity with respect to time, t, i.e. $a = \dfrac{dv}{dt}$.

45 Find $\displaystyle\int \frac{u^3 + 2}{u^3}\, du$.

> **Hint!**
> -
> Rearrange into a sum of terms before integrating.

3

46 Find the value of $\displaystyle\int_0^1 \sqrt{3x+1}\, dx$.

> **Hint!**
> -
> $$\int (ax+b)^n\, dx = \frac{(ax+b)^{n+1}}{a(n+1)} + c$$

5

47 Show that $\displaystyle\int_{\frac{\pi}{6}}^{\frac{5\pi}{12}} \cos\left(3\theta - \frac{\pi}{4}\right) d\theta = -\frac{\sqrt{2}}{6}$.

> **Hint!**
> -
> The integrals of $f(x) = \sin ax$ and $f(x) = \cos ax$
> are given in the Formulae list.

5

MARKS

48 The curve with equation $y = x^3 - 4x^2 + x + 6$ crosses the x-axis at the points A(-1, 0), B and C as shown in the diagram.

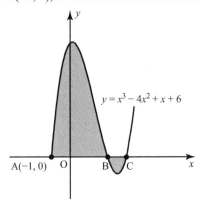

$y = x^3 - 4x^2 + x + 6$

A(-1, 0)   O   B C x

a) Find the coordinates of B and C.

b) Calculate the shaded area.

> **Hints!**
> a) Use a synthetic division table.
> b) Find the areas above and below the x-axis separately then add them together.

5

6

10

49 The diagram shows two curves with equations $y = \sin x$ and $y = \sin 2x$ for $0 \le x \le \pi$.

Calculate the shaded area.

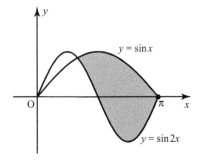

$y = \sin x$

O π x

$y = \sin 2x$

> **Hint!**
> Use $\int_a^b \text{upper} - \text{lower}$ where a and b are the points of intersection of the two curves.

4

50 The graph of $y = f(x)$ passes through the point $\left(\dfrac{\pi}{12}, 1 \right)$.

If $f'(x) = 3\cos 2x$, express y in terms of x.

> **Hint!**
> $y = \int \dfrac{dy}{dx}\, dx$

7

51 Water is being drained from a cylindrical tank.

The rate of change of the depth, d metres, of water in the tank is given by $d'(t) = 0.4 - k\sqrt{t}$.

t is the elapsed time, in minutes, since draining commenced.

k is a constant.

Initially the depth of the water was 3 metres.

The depth of the water was 1.2 metres after 9 seconds.

Express d in terms of t.

Algebraic and geometric skills

52 Two sequences are defined by these recurrence relations:

$u_{n+1} = 6u_n - 0.7$, $u_0 = 1$ and $v_{n+1} = 0.6v_n + 7$, $v_0 = 1$

a) Explain why only one of these sequences approaches a limit as $n \to \infty$.

b) Find the exact value of this limit.

c) For the other sequence, find

  i) the smallest term for which $u_n > 1000$ and

  ii) the value of n for that term

> **Hint!**
>
> If $-1 < a < 1$, $u_{n+1} = au_n + b$ converges to a limit
>
> given by $L = \dfrac{b}{1-a}$.

1

2

1

1

53 The first three terms of a sequence are 12, 15 and 19.

The sequence is generated by the recurrence relation $u_{n+1} = mu_n + c$.

Find the values of m and c.

> **Hint!**
>
> Form a pair of simultaneous equations.

4

54 A builders' merchant stocks bags of cement.

Each week it sells 80% of its stock and buys in 1400 new bags.

a) How many bags of cement will the merchant have in stock in the long run?

b) The merchant wants to reduce its long run stock level of cement.

Assuming that each week it continues to sell 80% of its stock, how many new bags should it buy in to maintain a long-run stock level of 1200 bags?

3

2

55 A recurrence relation is defined by $u_{n+1} = ku_n + 6$, $u_0 = 5$.

a) Find expressions for u_1 and u_2 in terms of k.

b) If $u_2 = 14$, find the value of k which produces a sequence with no limit.

2

4

56 The line L passes through the point $(2\sqrt{3},\ 1)$ and makes an angle of $\dfrac{\pi}{6}$ radians with the y-axis as shown in the diagram.

Find the equation of L.

3

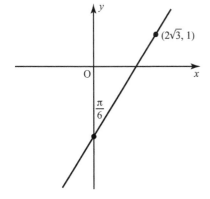

> **Hint!**
>
> If a line makes an angle of θ with the positive direction of the x-axis, then its gradient is equal to $\tan \theta$.

MARKS

57 A triangle ABC has vertices A(0, 7), B(8, −1) and C(−2, −3).

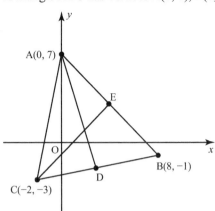

a) Find the equation of the median AD. **3**

b) Find the equation of the altitude CE. **3**

c) Find the coordinates of the point of intersection of AD and CE. **3**

> **Hints!**
>
> a) The median of a triangle is a straight line from a vertex to the midpoint of the opposite side.
>
> b) The altitude of a triangle is a straight line from a vertex perpendicular to the opposite side.
>
> c) Use simultaneous equations.

 58 ABCD is a kite with B the point (4, 8) and D the point (12, −4), as shown in the diagram.

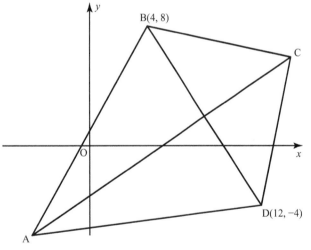

> **Hint!**
>
> One diagonal of a kite bisects the other at right angles.

a) Find the equation of the line AC, a diagonal of the kite. **4**

b) The line DC has equation $5x - y = 64$.

 i) Find the coordinates of the point C. **2**

 ii) Calculate the angle that DC makes with the positive direction of the x-axis. **2**

59 The point P(−1, 6) lies on the circle with equation
$x^2 + y^2 - 6x + 4y - 19 = 0$.

   a) Find the equation of the tangent to the circle at P.

   b) Show that the line with equation $y = x - 13$ is also a tangent to the circle and find the coordinates of the point of contact.

> *Hint!*
> --
> The tangent is the line through P(−1, 6) which is perpendicular to the radius hence
> $m_{\text{tangent}} \times m_{\text{radius}} = -1$.

4

5

60 Circles C_1 and C_2 have equations $(x - 5)^2 + (y + 10)^2 = 81$ and $x^2 + y^2 - 4y - 21 = 0$.

   a) Write down the centres and radii of C_1 and C_2.

   b) Show that C_1 and C_2 intersect.

> *Hint!*
> --
> Two circles intersect if the distance between their centres is less than the sum of their radii.

4

3

61 The centres A, B and C are collinear as shown.

The equations of the circumferences of the outer circles are $(x + 8)^2 + (y + 10)^2 = 256$ and $(x - 16)^2 + (y - 8)^2 = 36$.

Find the equation of the central circle.

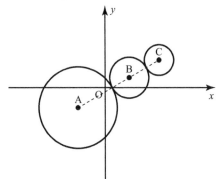

> *Hint!*
> --
> Start by finding the radii of the given circles and the distance between their centres.

7

62 Find the range of values of k for which the equation $x^2 + y^2 + 2kx - 4ky - 3k + 2 = 0$ represents a circle.

> *Hint!*
> --
> The equation $x^2 + y^2 + 2gx + 2fy + c = 0$ represents a circle provided that
> $g^2 + f^2 - c > 0$.

5

Algebraic and trigonometric skills

Question		Answer	Marks	Grade demand
1	a)	$5 - x = 0$ $\qquad x = 5$	State value.	C
	b)	$y = \dfrac{1}{5-x}$ $y(5-x) = 1$ $5 - x = \dfrac{1}{y}$ $x = 5 - \dfrac{1}{y}$ $f^{-1}(x) = 5 - \dfrac{1}{x}$ **OR** $f^{-1}(x) = \dfrac{5x-1}{x}$	Substitute y for $f(x)$ and start to rearrange. Complete rearrangement. State inverse function in terms of x. **4 marks**	C
2		$4 - x^2 \geq 0$ $x^2 \leq 4$ $-2 \leq x \leq 2$	Set denominator ≥ 0. Find suitable domain. **2 marks**	C
3	a)	$f\left(3\sin\dfrac{\pi}{6}\right) = f\left(\dfrac{3}{2}\right)$ $\qquad = 4 \times \dfrac{3}{2} = 6$	Evaluate expression.	C
	b)	$g(4x)$ $= 3\sin 4x$	Start composite process. Find $g(f(x))$. **3 marks**	C
4	a)	$f\left(2x + \dfrac{3}{2}\right)$ $= \dfrac{1}{2}\left(2x + \dfrac{3}{2}\right) - \dfrac{3}{4}$ $= x$	Start composite process. Find $g(f(x))$.	C
	b)	$g(x) = f^{-1}(x)$	State connection. **3 marks**	C
5	a)		Reflect in x-axis. Then vertical translation of 3 units up with all points correctly annotated.	C

Question		Answer	Marks	Grade demand
5	b)		Vertical stretch by factor 2. Then vertical translation of 1 unit down with all points correctly annotated.	C
	c)		Identify roots. Turning point at $-1 < x < 1$. Correct shape. **7 marks**	> C
6	a)		Horizontal compression by factor 2. Then vertical translation of 2 units up with all points correctly annotated.	C
	b)		Identify roots. Turning point at $(4, 0)$. Correct shape. **5 marks**	> C
7		amplitude $= \dfrac{2-(-4)}{2} \Rightarrow p = 3$ horizontal translation of 40° units right $\Rightarrow q = -40$ vertical translation of 1 unit up $\Rightarrow r = -1$	Find value of p. Find value of q. Find value of r. **3 marks**	> C

Question		Answer	Marks	Grade demand
8	a)	**Method 1** $\log_b x$ cuts x-axis at $(1, 0)$ hence $\log_b x \rightarrow \log_b(x + a)$ under horizontal translation of 3 units left $a = 3$ $b = 7$ **Method 2** $y = \log_b(x + a)$ $\log_b(-2 + a) = 0$ $-2 + a = b^0 = 1$ So $a = 3$ $1 = \log_b(4 + 3)$ $1 = \log_b 7$ $7 = b^1$ so $b = 7$	**Method 1** Identify relevant facts. State value of a. State value of b. **Method 2** Substitute $(-2, 0)$ into $y = \log_b(x + a)$. Find value of a. Find value of b.	> C
	b)	$x > -3$	State suitable domain.	> C
	c)		Reflect in $y = x$. Correct annotation and image asymptote shown. **6 marks**	> C
9		roots are -1 and 3 $\Rightarrow$ factors are $(x - 1)$ and $(x + 3)$ $\Rightarrow a = -1$ and $b = 3$ $(0, 3) \Rightarrow 3 = k \times (0 + 1) \times (0 - 3)$ $\qquad\qquad 3 = -3k$ $\qquad\qquad k = -1$	 Find values of a and b. Find value of k. **2 marks**	C
10	a)	$3(x^2 - 4x \ldots$ $3(x - 2)^2 \ldots$ $3(x - 2)^2 - 7$	Use common factor. Start to complete square. Complete process.	C
	b)	$f(x) \geq -7$	State range. **4 marks**	C

Question	Answer	Marks	Grade demand
11	$(2x-3)(x+4) \leq 0$ Zeros are $\dfrac{3}{2}$ and -4 Use a table of values or sketch graph of $y=(2x-3)(x+4)$ to find correct range of values. <table><tr><td>x</td><td>$\rightarrow$</td><td>-4</td><td>$\rightarrow$</td><td>$\dfrac{3}{2}$</td><td>$\rightarrow$</td></tr><tr><td>$2x^2+5x-12$</td><td>$+$</td><td>0</td><td>$-$</td><td>0</td><td>$+$</td></tr></table> $-4 \leq x \leq \dfrac{3}{2}$	Find zeros. Find correct range of values. **2 marks**	C
12	$b^2-4ac = k^2-4\times2\times k$ $\qquad\qquad = k^2+8k$ $\qquad\qquad = k(k+8)$ Zeros are 0 and -8 $k^2-4\times2\times(-k)<0$ <table><tr><td>x</td><td>$\rightarrow$</td><td>-8</td><td>$\rightarrow$</td><td>0</td><td>$\rightarrow$</td></tr><tr><td>k^2+8k</td><td>$+$</td><td>0</td><td>$-$</td><td>0</td><td>$+$</td></tr></table> $-8<k<0$	Use the discriminant Identify zeros of quadratic expression Apply $b^2-4ac>0$ State range with justification **4 marks**	> C

Question		Answer	Marks	Grade demand
13	a)	$kx^2 + 3x + 3 = k$	Substitute $y = k$ into equation of parabola.	> C
		$kx^2 + 3x + (3 - k) = 0$	Rearrange into standard quadratic form.	
		$b^2 - 4ac = 9 - 4k(3 - k)$	Use discriminant	
		$9 - 12k - 4k^2 = 0$	Apply $b^2 - 4ac = 0$	
		$(3 - 2k)^2 = 0$		
		$k = \dfrac{3}{2}$	Solve for k.	
	b)	For all real values of k, $(3 - 2k)^2 \geq 0$ so the equation $kx^2 + 3x + 3 = k$ has one or two real roots so the line and parabola touch or intersect.	State discriminant ≥ 0. Complete justification. **7 marks**	> C
14	a)	$\begin{array}{c|ccccc} 3 & 2 & -1 & -14 & -5 & 6 \\ & & & & & \\ \hline & 2 & & & & \end{array}$ $\begin{array}{c|ccccc} 3 & 2 & -1 & -14 & -5 & 6 \\ & & 6 & 15 & 3 & -6 \\ \hline & 2 & 5 & 1 & -2 & \big| \; 0 \end{array}$ $f(3) = 0 \Rightarrow x = 3$ is a root	Use $x = 3$ in synthetic division table. Complete division, interpret result and state conclusion.	> C
	b)	$(x - 3)(2x^3 + 5x + x - 2) = 0$ $\begin{array}{c|cccc} -1 & 2 & 5 & -1 & -2 \\ & & -2 & 3 & 2 \\ \hline & 2 & 3 & 2 & \big| \; 0 \end{array}$ $(x - 3)(x + 1)(2x^2 + 3x - 2) = 0$ $(x - 3)(x + 1)(x + 2)(2x - 1) = 0$ Other roots are $x = -1, -2, \dfrac{1}{2}$	State cubic factor. Find quadratic factor. Factorise completely. State other roots. **6 marks**	> C
15		$\begin{array}{c|cccc} 2 & 1 & p & q & -12 \\ & & 2 & 2p + 4 & 4p + 2q + 8 \\ \hline & 1 & p + 2 & 2p + q + 4 & \big| \; 4p + 2q - 4 \end{array}$ $4p + 2q - 4 = 10$, so $4p + 2q = 14 \Leftrightarrow 2p + q = 7$ $\begin{array}{c|cccc} 1 & 1 & p & q & -12 \\ & & 1 & p + 1 & p + q + 1 \\ \hline & 1 & p + 1 & p + q + 1 & \big| \; p + q - 11 \end{array}$ $p + q - 11 = 0$, so $p + q = 11$ $\begin{array}{r} 2p + q = 7 \\ - \quad p + q = 11 \\ \hline p \qquad = -4 \end{array}$ $\qquad q = 15$	Use $x = 2$ in synthetic division table to obtain equation. Use $x = 1$ in synthetic division table to obtain equation. Use simultaneous equations. Find values of p and q. **4 marks**	> C

Question		Answer	Marks	Grade demand
16	**a)**	$x^3 - 12x + 1 = 5x^2 - 15x - 8$	Form equation and rearrange into standard cubic form.	> C
		$x^3 - 5x^2 + 3x + 9 = 0$		
		$\begin{array}{c\|cccc} -1 & 1 & -5 & 3 & 9 \\ & & & & \\ \hline & 1 & & & \end{array}$	Use $x = -1$ in synthetic division table.	
		$\begin{array}{c\|cccc} -1 & 1 & -5 & 3 & 9 \\ & & -1 & 6 & -9 \\ \hline & 1 & -6 & 9 & \;\vline\; 0 \end{array}$		
		$f(-1) = 0 \Rightarrow x = -1$ is a root so the curves meet at the point where $x = -1$	Complete division, interpret result and state conclusion.	
	b)	$(x+1)(x^2 - 6x + 9) = 0$	State quadratic factor.	> C
		$(x+1)(x-3)^2 = 0$	Factorise completely.	
		$x = -1, \; x = 3$	Find x-coordinates of points of intersection.	
		$x = -1 \Rightarrow y = (-1)^3 - 12 \times (-1) + 1 = 12$		
		$x = 3 \Rightarrow y = 3^3 - 12 \times 3 + 1 = -8$		
		Points of intersection are $(-1, 12)$ and $(3, -8)$	State coordinates of points of intersection.	
			7 marks	
17		$\log_6 16^{\frac{1}{2}} + \log_6 9 = \log_6 4 + \log_6 9$	Apply $n \log ax = \log_a x^n$.	C
		$= \log_6 36$	Apply $\log_a x + \log_a y = \log_a xy$.	
		$= 2$	Evaluate logarithm.	
			3 marks	
18		$\log_a 10^3 - \log_a 500 = \frac{1}{3}$		C
		$\log_a 1000 - \log_a 500 = \frac{1}{3}$	Apply $n \log ax = \log_a x^n$.	
		$\log_a 2 = \frac{1}{3}$	Apply $\log_a x - \log_a y = \log_a \frac{x}{y}$.	
		$a^{\frac{1}{3}} = 2$	Write in exponential form.	
		$a = 2^3 = 8$	Find value of a.	
			4 marks	
19		$\log_2 (x-6)(x+1) = 3$	Apply $\log_a x + \log_a y = \log_a xy$.	C
		$\log_2 (x^2 - 5x - 6) = 3$	Write in exponential form.	
		$(x-6)(x+1) = 2^3$		
		$x^2 - 5x - 6 = 8$		
		$x^2 - 5x - 14 = 0$	Write in standard quadratic form.	
		$(x-7)(x+2) = 0$		
		$x = 7, x = -2$		
		$x = 7$ since $x > 6$	Solve for x and identify appropriate solution.	
			4 marks	

Question		Answer	Marks	Grade demand
20	a)	$80 = 100e^{-10k}$	Substitute for T_t, T_0 and t in formula.	> C
		$e^{-10k} = 0.8$		
		$-10k = \ln 0.8$	Write in logarithmic form.	
		$k = \dfrac{\ln 0.8}{-10} = 0.0223\ldots$	Solve to find k.	
	b)	$T = 80e^{-0.0223\ldots \times 30}$	Substitute for T_0, k and t in formula.	> C
		$= 41\ldots$	Evaluate formula and find required answer.	
		So the temperature has dropped by 39 in the next half hour.	**5 marks**	
21		**Method 1**	**Method 1**	> C
		$\log_3 y = \log_3 kx^n$	Take logarithms of both sides of equation.	
		$\log_3 y = \log_3 x^n + \log_3 k$	Apply $\log_a xy = \log_a x + \log_a y$.	
		$\log_3 y = n\log_3 x + \log_3 k$	Apply $\log_a x^n = n\log ax$.	
		y-intercept $= 2 = \log_3 k$		
		$k = 3^2 = 9$	Find k.	
		gradient $= -\dfrac{1}{4} = n$	Find n.	
		Method 2	**Method 2**	
		$\log_3 y = -\dfrac{1}{4}\log_3 x + 2$	State linear equation.	
		$\log_3 y = -\dfrac{1}{4}\log_3 x + \log_3 3^2$		
		$\log_3 y = -\dfrac{1}{4}\log_3 x + \log_3 9$	Express all terms in terms of $\log_3$.	
		$\log_3 y = \log_3 x^{-\frac{1}{4}} + \log_3 9$	Use $n\log ax = \log_a x^n$.	
		$\log_3 y = \log_3 9x^{-\frac{1}{4}}$	Use $\log_a x + \log_a y = \log_a xy$.	
		$y = 9x^{-\frac{1}{4}}$	Interpret result.	
			5 marks	

Question	Answer	Marks	Grade demand
22	**Method 1** $\log_4 y = \log_4 ab^x$ $\log_4 y = \log_4 b^x + \log_4 a$ $\log_4 y = x\log_4 b + \log_4 a$ $\log_4 a = 1$ $\quad a = 4^1 = 4$ $\log_4 b = \dfrac{3}{2}$ $b = 4^{\frac{3}{2}} = 8$ **Method 2** $\log_4 y = \dfrac{3}{2}x + 1$ $\quad y = 4^{\frac{3}{2}x+1}$ $\quad y = 4^{\frac{3}{2}x}4^1$ $a = 4^1 = 4$ $b = 4^{\frac{3}{2}} = 8$	**Method 1** Take logarithms of both sides of equation. Apply $\log_a xy = \log_a x + \log_a y$. Apply $\log_a x^n = n\log ax$. Find a. Find b. **Method 2** Use equation of line. Write in exponential form. Apply $x^{m+n} = x^m \times x^n$. Find a. Find b. **5 marks**	> C
23	$OA = \sqrt{5^2 + 12^2} = 13$ $OB = \sqrt{8^2 + 6^2} = 10$ $\sin AOB = \sin(p - q)$ $\qquad = \sin p\cos q - \cos p\sin q$ $\qquad = \dfrac{12}{13}\times\dfrac{8}{10} - \dfrac{5}{13}\times\dfrac{6}{10}$ $\qquad = \dfrac{66}{130}$ $\qquad = \dfrac{33}{65}$	Find the length of hypotenuse of both triangles. Use appropriate addition formula. Find two of $\sin p$, $\sin q$, $\cos p$, $\cos q$. Find other two and substitute into formula. Find value of $\sin AOB$ in simplest form. **5 marks**	C
24	$\sin 2x = 2\sin x\cos x$ $\qquad = 2\times\dfrac{1}{\sqrt{8}}\times\dfrac{\sqrt{7}}{\sqrt{8}}$ $\qquad = \dfrac{2\sqrt{7}}{8}$ $\qquad = \dfrac{\sqrt{7}}{4}$ $\cos 2x = \cos^2 x - \sin^2 x$ $\qquad = \left(\dfrac{\sqrt{7}}{\sqrt{8}}\right)^2 - \left(\dfrac{1}{\sqrt{8}}\right)^2$ $\qquad = \dfrac{7}{8} - \dfrac{1}{8} = \dfrac{6}{8} = \dfrac{3}{4}$	Expand $\sin 2x$. Substitute exact values of $\sin x$ and $\cos x$. Find exact value of $\sin 2x$ in simplest form. Expand $\cos 2x$ and substitute exact values of $\sin x$ and $\cos x$. Find exact value of $\cos 2x$ in simplest form. **5 marks**	C

Question		Answer	Marks	Grade demand
25		$\cos 3x° = -\dfrac{1}{2}$	Solve for $\cos 3x$.	> C
		$3x = 120, 300, 480$	Find all solutions for $3x$ or two solutions for x.	
		$x = 40, 100, 160$	Find all solutions for x.	
			3 marks	
26		$1 - 2\sin^2 \theta + \sin \theta = 0$	Use appropriate formula for $\cos 2\theta$.	> C
		$2\sin^2 \theta - \sin \theta - 1 = 0$	Rearrange into standard quadratic form.	
		$(2\sin \theta + 1)(\sin \theta - 1) = 0$	Factorise.	
		$\sin \theta = -\dfrac{1}{2},\ \sin \theta = 1$	Find both solutions for $\sin \theta$ or two solutions for θ.	
		$\theta = \dfrac{7\pi}{6}, \dfrac{11\pi}{6}; \theta = \dfrac{\pi}{2}$	Find all solutions for θ.	
			5 marks	
27		$\dfrac{2\sin x \cos x}{1 + \cos 2x}$	Use formula for $\sin 2x$.	> C
		$= \dfrac{2\sin x \cos x}{1 + 2\cos^2 x - 1}$	Use appropriate formula for $\cos 2x$.	
		$= \dfrac{2\sin x \cos x}{2\cos^2 x}$	Show remaining steps to obtain required answer.	
		$= \dfrac{\sin x}{\cos x}$		
		$= \tan x$	**3 marks**	
28	a)	$4\cos x° + \sin x° = k(\cos x° \cos a° + \sin x° \sin a°)$	Use addition formula.	C
		$k\cos a° = 4,\ k\sin a° = 1$	Equate coefficients.	
		$k = \sqrt{1^2 + 4^2} = \sqrt{17}$	Find k.	
		$a = \tan^{-1}\left(\dfrac{1}{4}\right) = 14$		
		$4\cos x° + \sin x° = \sqrt{17}\cos(x - 14)°$	Find a and state expression in required form.	
	b)	$\sqrt{17}\cos(x - 14)° + \sqrt{13} = 0$	Link to (a)	> C
		$\cos(x - 14)° = \dfrac{-\sqrt{13}}{\sqrt{17}}$		
		$x - 14 = 151, 209$	Solve for $x - 14$.	
		$x = 165, 223$	Solve for x.	
			7 marks	

Question	Answer	Marks	Grade demand
29 a)	$\sqrt{3}\sin x - \cos x = k(\sin x\cos a - \cos x\sin a)$ $k\cos a = \sqrt{3},\ k\sin a = 1$ $k = \sqrt{1^2 + \sqrt{3}^2} = 2$ $a = \tan^{-1}\left(\dfrac{1}{\sqrt{3}}\right) = \dfrac{\pi}{6}$ $\sin x - \sqrt{3}\cos x = 2\sin\left(x - \dfrac{\pi}{6}\right)$	Use addition formula. Equate coefficients. Find k. Find a and state expression in required form.	C
b)		Maximum t.p. $\left(\dfrac{2\pi}{3}, 2\right)$ and minimum t.p. $\left(\dfrac{5\pi}{3}, -2\right)$. x-intercepts $\left(\dfrac{\pi}{6}, 0\right)$ and $\left(\dfrac{7\pi}{6}, 0\right)$. Endpoints $\left(0, -\sqrt{3}\right)$ and $\left(2\pi, -\sqrt{3}\right)$. **7 marks**	> C

Geometric skills

Question	Answer	Marks	Grade demand
30	$\overrightarrow{PQ} = \begin{pmatrix} 4 \\ 6 \\ -2 \end{pmatrix}$ $\overrightarrow{QR} = \begin{pmatrix} 6 \\ 9 \\ -3 \end{pmatrix}$ $\Rightarrow \overrightarrow{QR} = \dfrac{3}{2}\overrightarrow{PQ}$ So PQ and QR are parallel, and since Q is a common point, then P, Q and R are collinear. $PQ:QR = 2:3$	Find the components of $\overrightarrow{PQ}$. Find components of $\overrightarrow{QR}$ and express as a multiple of $\overrightarrow{PQ}$. State conclusion with justification. State ratio. **4 marks**	C
31	$\overrightarrow{AB} = \dfrac{2}{3}\overrightarrow{AC}$ $\mathbf{b} - \mathbf{a} = \dfrac{2}{3}(\mathbf{c} - \mathbf{a})$ $\mathbf{b} = \dfrac{1}{3}(2\mathbf{c} + \mathbf{a})$ $\mathbf{b} = \dfrac{1}{3}\left(\begin{pmatrix} 10 \\ 4 \\ -2 \end{pmatrix} + \begin{pmatrix} -1 \\ -7 \\ 8 \end{pmatrix} \right)$ $B(3, -1, 2)$	Interpret ratio. Find coordinates of B. **2 marks**	C
32 a)	$\overrightarrow{AM} = \overrightarrow{AD} + \overrightarrow{DH} + \overrightarrow{HM}$ $\quad = \overrightarrow{AD} + \overrightarrow{AE} + \dfrac{1}{2}\overrightarrow{AB}$ $\overrightarrow{AM} = \begin{pmatrix} -3 \\ 4 \\ 8 \end{pmatrix}$	Express $\overrightarrow{AM}$ in terms of $\overrightarrow{AB}$, $\overrightarrow{AD}$ and $\overrightarrow{AE}$. Find components of $\overrightarrow{AM}$.	C
32 b)	$\overrightarrow{AN} = \overrightarrow{AB} + \overrightarrow{BF} + \overrightarrow{FN}$ $\quad = \overrightarrow{AB} + \overrightarrow{AE} + \dfrac{1}{3}\overrightarrow{AD}$ $\overrightarrow{AN} = \begin{pmatrix} 2 \\ 4 \\ 6 \end{pmatrix}$	Express $\overrightarrow{AN}$ in terms of $\overrightarrow{AB}$, $\overrightarrow{AD}$ and $\overrightarrow{AE}$. Find components of $\overrightarrow{AN}$.	C

Question		Answer	Marks	Grade demand
32	c)	$\overrightarrow{AM}.\overrightarrow{AN}=58$	Evaluate $\overrightarrow{DA}.\overrightarrow{AE}$	C
		$\left\|\overrightarrow{AM}\right\|=\sqrt{89}$ and $\left\|\overrightarrow{AN}\right\|=\sqrt{56}$	Evaluate $\left\|\overrightarrow{DA}\right\|$ and $\left\|\overrightarrow{AE}\right\|$	
			Use scalar product	
		$\cos MAN = \dfrac{58}{\sqrt{89}\sqrt{56}}$		
		angle $MAN = 34 \cdot 8°$	Calculate angle	
			8 marks	
33		$\mathbf{u}.\mathbf{v} = 2\times3+0\times4+6\times-1=0$	Find value of $\mathbf{u}.\mathbf{v}$.	C
		$\mathbf{u}$ and $\mathbf{v}$ are perpendicular since $\mathbf{u}.\mathbf{v}=0$	State conclusion with justification.	
			2 marks	
34		$\sqrt{8^2+(-\sqrt{5})^2+(2\sqrt{3})^2}$	Start to find magnitude of $\mathbf{a}$.	C
		$=\sqrt{64+5+12}$		
		$=\sqrt{81}=9$	Find magnitude of $\mathbf{a}$.	
		$k=\dfrac{1}{9}$	Find value of k.	
			3 marks	
35		$\mathbf{p}.\mathbf{q}+\mathbf{p}.\mathbf{r}$	Expand brackets.	> C
		$\mathbf{p}.\mathbf{q}=5\times5\times\cos90°$ $\mathbf{p}.\mathbf{r}=5\times5\times\cos60°$	Start to evaluate $\mathbf{p}.\mathbf{q}$ and $\mathbf{p}.\mathbf{r}$.	
		$\mathbf{p}.\mathbf{q}+\mathbf{p}.\mathbf{r}=25\times0+25\times\dfrac{1}{2}=\dfrac{25}{2}$	Evaluate $\mathbf{p}.\mathbf{q}+\mathbf{p}.\mathbf{r}$.	
			3 marks	

Calculus skills

Question		Answer	Marks	Grade demand
36		$y = 2x^{\frac{3}{2}} - 2x^{\frac{1}{2}} + 3\cos 2x$	Multiply out brackets.	C
		$\dfrac{dy}{dx} = 3x^{\frac{1}{2}} \ldots$	Differentiate first term.	
		$= 3x^{\frac{1}{2}} - x^{-\frac{1}{2}} \ldots$	Differentiate second term.	
		$= 3x^{\frac{1}{2}} - x^{-\frac{1}{2}} - 3\sin 2x \ldots$	Start to differentiate third term.	
		$= 3x^{\frac{1}{2}} - x^{-\frac{1}{2}} - 6\sin 2x$	Complete differentiation of third term. **5 marks**	
37		$f'(x) = 4\left(3 - x^2\right)^3 \ldots$	Start to differentiate.	> C
		$= 4\left(3 - x^2\right)^3 \times -2x$	Complete differentiation.	
		$= -8x\left(3 - x^2\right)^3$		
		$f'(2) = -8 \times 2 \times \left(3 - 2^2\right)^3$	Evaluate $f'(2)$.	
		$= -16 \times \left(-1\right)^3$		
		$= 16$	**3 marks**	
38		$P = 3(1 - 4n)^{-1}$	Prepare to differentiate.	> C
		$\dfrac{dP}{dn} = -3(1 - 4n)^{-2} \ldots$	Start to differentiate.	
		$= -3(1 - 4n)^{-2} \times -4$	Complete differentiation.	
		$= 12(1 - 4n)^{-2}$	**3 marks**	
39		$f'(x) = \cos\left(2x + \pi\right) \ldots$	Start to differentiate first term.	> C
		$= 2\cos\left(2x + \pi\right) \ldots$	Complete differentiation of first term.	
		$= 2\cos\left(2x + \pi\right) - 3\cos^2 x \ldots$	Start to differentiate second term.	
		$= 2\cos\left(2x + \pi\right) + 3\cos^2 x \sin x$	Complete differentiation of second term. **4 marks**	
40	a)	$f'(x) = 2x^2 + 6x - 8$	Differentiate.	C
		at $x = -3$ $f'(-3) = 2(-3)^2 + 6(-3) - 8 = -8$	Evaluate derivative.	
		$y = \dfrac{2}{3}(-3)^3 + 3(-3)^2 - 8(-3) + 1 = 34$	Evaluate y-coordinate.	
		$y - 34 = -8(x - (-3))$	Find equation of tangent.	
		$\Leftrightarrow y = -8x + 10$		

Question		Answer	Marks	Grade demand
40	b)	$2x^2 + 6x - 8 < 0$ $2(x^2 + 3x - 4) < 0$ $2(x + 4)(x - 1) < 0$ Use a table of values or sketch graph of $y = (x + 4)(x - 1)$ to find correct range of values.	Set derivative < 0. Find zeros.	C

x	$\rightarrow$	-4	$\rightarrow$	1	$\rightarrow$
$f'(x)$	$+$	0	$-$	0	$+$

Find correct range of values.

Zeros are -4 and 1.

$-4 < x < 1$

7 marks

| 41 | a) | $(0, -20)$
 $(2, 0)$ and $(5, 0)$ | Find y-intercept.
 Find x-intercepts. | C |
| | b) | $f(x) = x^3 - 9x^2 + 24x - 20$
 $f'(x) = 3x^2 - 18x + 24$

 $3x^2 - 18x + 24 = 0$
 $3(x^2 - 6x + 8) = 0$
 $3(x - 2)(x - 4) = 0$

 $x = 2, \ x = 4$
 $x = 2 \Rightarrow y = 0$
 $x = 4 \Rightarrow y = -4$ | Prepare to differentiate.
 Differentiate.

 Set derivative equal to zero.

 Find x-coordinates.
 Find y-coordinates. | C |

x	$\rightarrow$	2	$\rightarrow$	4	$\rightarrow$
$f'(x)$	$-$	0	$+$	0	$+$
slope	╱	—	╲	—	╱

Determine nature of stationary points.

$(2, 0)$ is a maximum turning point.

$(4, -4)$ is a minimum turning point.

State nature of stationary points.

Question		Answer	Marks	Grade demand
41	c)		Sketch curve. **10 marks**	C
42		$f'(x) = 3x^2 - 4x - 7$ $3x^2 - 4x - 7 = 0$ $(3x - 7)(x + 1) = 0$ $x = \dfrac{7}{3}, x = -1$ $f(-1) = -1 - 2 + 7 + 1 = 5$ $f(-2) = -8 - 8 + 14 + 1 = -1$ $f(2) = 8 - 8 - 14 + 1 = -13$ Maximum = 5, minimum = -13	Differentiate. Set derivative equal to zero. Factorise derivative. Solve equation. Evaluate f at relevant stationary point. Evaluate f at endpoints of interval. State maximum and minimum values. **7 marks**	> C
43		$V = 4x^2 h = 800$ $h = \dfrac{800}{4x^2} = \dfrac{200}{x^2}$ $A(x) = 8x^2 + 10xh$ $= 8x^2 + 10x \times \dfrac{200}{x^2}$ $= 8x^2 + \dfrac{2000}{x}$ $A(x) = 8x^2 + 2000x^{-1}$ $A'(x) = 16x - 2000x^{-2}$ $16x - 2000x^{-2} = 0$ $16x = \dfrac{2000}{x^2}$ $x^3 = 125$ $x = 5$ (sign table) Hence the surface area of the cuboid is minimised when $x = 5$.	Find expression for h in terms of x. Find formula for surface area. Show steps leading to given formula for surface area. Prepare to differentiate. Differentiate. Set derivative equal to zero. Solve for x. Justify nature of stationary point. **8 marks**	> C

Sign table for Question 43:

x		$\rightarrow$	5	$\rightarrow$
$A'(x)$		$-$	0	$+$
slope		↘	—	↗

Question	Answer	Marks	Grade demand
44	$s = (6 \times 4 + 1)^{\frac{3}{2}} = \sqrt{25^3} = 125 \text{ m}$	Evaluate s when $t = 4$.	$> C$
	$v = \dfrac{ds}{dt} = \dfrac{3}{2}(6t+1)^{\frac{1}{2}} \ldots$	Start to differentiate s with respect to t.	
	$= \dfrac{3}{2}(6t+1)^{\frac{1}{2}} \times 6 = 9(6t+1)^{\frac{1}{2}}$	Complete differentiation.	
		Evaluate v when $t = 4$.	
	$9(6 \times 4 + 1)^{\frac{1}{2}} = 9 \times \sqrt{25} = 45 \text{ ms}^{-1}$		
	$a = \dfrac{dv}{dt} = 27(6t+1)^{-\frac{1}{2}}$	Differentiate v with respect to t.	
		Evaluate a when $t = 4$.	
	$27(6 \times 4 + 1)^{-\frac{1}{2}} = \dfrac{27}{\sqrt{25}} = \dfrac{27}{5} \text{ ms}^{-2}$	**6 marks**	
45	$\int 1 + 2u^{-3}\, du$	Prepare to integrate.	C
	$= u \ldots$	Integrate first term.	
	$= u - u^{-2} + c$	Integrate second term and add constant of integration. **3 marks**	
46	$\displaystyle\int_0^1 (3x+1)^{\frac{1}{2}}\, dx$	Prepare to integrate.	$> C$
	$\left[\dfrac{(3x+1)^{\frac{3}{2}}}{\frac{3}{2}} \ldots \right]_0^1$	Start to integrate.	
	$\left[\dfrac{(3x+1)^{\frac{3}{2}}}{\frac{3}{2} \times 3} \right]_0^1$	Process coefficient of x.	
	$= \left(\dfrac{2(3 \times 1 + 1)^{\frac{3}{2}}}{9} \right) - \left(\dfrac{2(3 \times 0 + 1)^{\frac{3}{2}}}{9} \right)$	Substitute limits.	
	$= \left(\dfrac{2 \times 4^{\frac{3}{2}}}{9} \right) - \left(\dfrac{2 \times 1^{\frac{3}{2}}}{9} \right)$		
	$= \left(\dfrac{2 \times 8}{9} \right) - \left(\dfrac{2 \times 1}{9} \right)$		
	$= \dfrac{16}{9} - \dfrac{2}{9} = \dfrac{14}{9}$	Evaluate integral. **5 marks**	

Question	Answer	Marks	Grade demand
47	$\left[...\sin(3\theta - \dfrac{\pi}{4})\right]_{\frac{\pi}{6}}^{\frac{5\pi}{12}}$	Start to integrate.	> C
	$\left[\dfrac{1}{3}\sin(3\theta - \dfrac{\pi}{4})\right]_{\frac{\pi}{6}}^{\frac{5\pi}{12}}$	Process coefficient of θ.	
	$= \dfrac{1}{3}\sin\left(\dfrac{15\pi}{12} - \dfrac{\pi}{4}\right) - \dfrac{1}{3}\sin\left(\dfrac{3\pi}{6} - \dfrac{\pi}{4}\right)$	Substitute limits.	
	$= \dfrac{1}{3}\sin\pi - \dfrac{1}{3}\sin\dfrac{\pi}{4} = \dfrac{1}{3}\times 0 - \dfrac{1}{3}\times\dfrac{1}{\sqrt{2}}$		
	$= -\dfrac{1}{3\sqrt{2}}$	Evaluate integral.	
	$= -\dfrac{1}{3\sqrt{2}}\times\dfrac{\sqrt{2}}{\sqrt{2}}$		
	$= -\dfrac{\sqrt{2}}{6}$	Rearrange into required form. **5 marks**	
48 a)	$\begin{array}{r|rrrr} -1 & 1 & -4 & 1 & 9 \\ & & & & \\ \hline & 1 & & & \end{array}$	Use $x = -1$ in synthetic division table.	C
	$\begin{array}{r|rrrr} -1 & 1 & -4 & 1 & 6 \\ & & -1 & 5 & -6 \\ \hline & 1 & -5 & 6 & 0 \end{array}$	Complete division.	
	$(x+1)(x^2 - 5x + 6) = 0$	Find quadratic factor.	
	$(x+1)(x-2)(x-3) = 0$	Factorise completely.	
	$x = -1, 2, 3$		
	$B(2, 0)$ and $C(3, 0)$	State coordinates of B and C.	
b)	$\displaystyle\int_{-1}^{2}(x^3 - 4x^2 + x + 6)\,dx$	Correct integral for area above x-axis.	C
	$= \left[\dfrac{x^4}{4} - \dfrac{4x^3}{3} + \dfrac{x^2}{2} + 6x\right]_{-1}^{2}$	Integrate.	
	$= \left(4 - \dfrac{4\times 8}{3} + 2 + 12\right) -$	Substitute limits.	
	$\left(\dfrac{1}{4} - \dfrac{(-4)}{3} + \dfrac{1}{2} + (-6)\right)$		
	$= 11\dfrac{1}{4}$	Evaluate area above x-axis.	
	$= \left[\dfrac{x^4}{4} - \dfrac{4x^3}{3} + \dfrac{x^2}{2} + 6x\right]_{2}^{3}$	Substitute limits for area below x-axis.	
	$= \left(\dfrac{81}{4} - \dfrac{4\times 27}{3} + \dfrac{9}{2} + 18\right) -$		
	$\left(16 - \dfrac{4\times 8}{3} + 4 + 12\right) = -\dfrac{7}{12}$		
	Total area $= 11\dfrac{1}{4} + \dfrac{7}{12} = 11\dfrac{5}{6}$	Find total area. **11 marks**	

Question	Answer	Marks	Grade demand
49	$\sin 2x = \sin x$	Form equation to find limits.	> C
	$2\sin x \cos x = \sin x$	Use double angle formula.	
	$2\sin x \cos x - \sin x = 0$		
	$\sin x\,(2\cos x - 1) = 0$	Rearrange and factorise.	
	$\sin x = 0, \cos x = \dfrac{1}{2}$	Solve for $\sin x$ and $\cos x$.	
	$x = \pi, \dfrac{\pi}{3}$	Solve for required x.	
	$\displaystyle\int_{\frac{\pi}{3}}^{\pi} (\sin x - \sin 2x)\,dx$	Correct integral for area.	
	$= \Big[-\cos x + \cos 2x \ldots\Big]_{\frac{\pi}{3}}^{\pi}$	Start to integrate.	
	$= \left[-\cos x + \dfrac{1}{2}\cos 2x\right]_{\frac{\pi}{3}}^{\pi}$	Process coefficient of x.	
	$= \left(-\cos \pi + \dfrac{1}{2}\cos 2\pi\right)$ $\quad - \left(-\cos\dfrac{\pi}{3} + \dfrac{1}{2}\cos\left(2\times\dfrac{\pi}{3}\right)\right)$	Substitute limits.	
	$= \left(1 + \dfrac{1}{2}\right) - \left(-\dfrac{1}{2} - \dfrac{1}{4}\right)$		
	$= \dfrac{9}{4}$	Find area.	
		10 marks	
50	$y = \displaystyle\int (3\cos 2x)\,dx$	Know to integrate.	C
	$= \dfrac{3}{2}\sin 2x + c$	Integrate.	
	$1 = \dfrac{3}{2}\sin\left(2\times\dfrac{\pi}{12}\right) + c$	Substitute for x and y.	
	$\Leftrightarrow 1 = \dfrac{3}{2}\times\dfrac{1}{2} + c$		
	$\Rightarrow c = \dfrac{1}{4}$		
	$y = \dfrac{3}{2}\sin 2x + \dfrac{1}{4}$	Express y in terms of x.	
		4 marks	

Question	Answer	Marks	Grade demand
51	$d = \int (0{\cdot}4 - k\sqrt{t})\,dt$	Know to integrate.	$> C$
	$= \int \left(0{\cdot}4 - kt^{\frac{1}{2}}\right) dt$	Prepare to integrate.	
	$= 0{\cdot}4t \dots$	Integrate first term.	
	$= 0{\cdot}4t - \dfrac{kt^{\frac{3}{2}}}{\frac{3}{2}} + c$	Integrate second term.	
	$3 = 0{\cdot}4 \times 0 - \dfrac{2}{3}k \times 0^{\frac{3}{2}} + c$		
	$c = 3$	Find constant of integration.	
	$d = 0{\cdot}4t - \dfrac{2}{3}kt^{\frac{3}{2}} + 3$		
	$1{\cdot}2 = 0{\cdot}4 \times 9 - \dfrac{2}{3}k \times 9^{\frac{3}{2}} + 3$		
	$1{\cdot}2 = 3{\cdot}6 - 18k + 3$		
	$18k = 5{\cdot}4$		
	$k = 0{\cdot}3$	Find value of k.	
		Express d in terms of t.	
	$d = 0{\cdot}4t - 0{\cdot}2t^{\frac{3}{2}} + 3$	**7 marks**	

Algebraic and geometric skills

Question			Answer	Marks	Grade demand
52	a)		$a_u = 6 \Rightarrow a_u > 1$ $\Rightarrow$ no limit $a_v = 0 \cdot 6 \Rightarrow -1 < a_v < 1$ $\Rightarrow$ converges to a limit	Explanation.	C
	b)		$L = \dfrac{7}{1 - 0 \cdot 6}$ $= \dfrac{7}{0 \cdot 4} = \dfrac{70}{4} = \dfrac{35}{2}$	Substitute into limit formula. Calculate limit.	C C
	c)	i)	$u_1 = 5 \cdot 3, \ u_2 = 31 \cdot 1, \ u_3 = 185 \cdot 9$ $u_4 = 1114 \cdot 7$	Find value of u_4.	C
		ii)	$n = 4$	State value of n. <div align="right">**5 marks**</div>	C
53			$15 = 12m + c$ $19 = 15m + c$ $4 = 3m$ $m = \dfrac{4}{3}$ $15 = \dfrac{4}{3} \times 12 + c$ $15 = 16 + c$ $c = -1$	Form equation connecting u_0 and u_1. Form equation connecting u_1 and u_2. Find value of m. Find value of c. <div align="right">**4 marks**</div>	C
54	a)		$u_{n+1} = 0 \cdot 2 u_n + \ldots$ $u_{n+1} = 0 \cdot 2 u_n + 1400$ $L = \dfrac{1400}{1 - 0 \cdot 2} = 1750$	Start recurrence relation. Complete recurrence relation. Calculate limit.	> C
	b)		$1200 = \dfrac{b}{1 - 0 \cdot 2}$ $b = 1200 \times (1 - 0 \cdot 2) = 960$ bags	Substitute into limit formula. Calculate number of bags. <div align="right">**5 marks**</div>	> C

Question		Answer	Marks	Grade demand
55	a)	$u_1 = 5k + 6$	Find expression for u_1.	> C
		$u_2 = k(5k+6) + 6$	Find expression for u_2.	
		$= 5k^2 + 6k + 6$		
	b)	$5k^2 + 6k + 6 = 14$	Interpret information.	
		$5k^2 + 6k - 8 = 0$	Express equation in standard quadratic form.	
		$(5k - 4)(k + 2) = 0$		
		$k = \dfrac{4}{5}, k = -2$	Find zeros.	
			State value of k with justification.	
		$k = \dfrac{4}{5}$ produces a sequence with no limit as $-1 < k < 1$ for a limit to exist.	**6 marks**	
56		$m = \tan\dfrac{\pi}{3}$	Know how to find gradient of line.	> C
		$= \sqrt{3}$	Find gradient of line.	
		$y - 1 = \sqrt{3}(x - 2\sqrt{3})$		
		$y - 1 = \sqrt{3}x - 6$		
		$y = \sqrt{3}x - 5$ or equivalent	Find equation of line.	
			3 marks	
57	a)	$D(3, -2)$	Calculate midpoint of BC.	C
		$m_{AD} = \dfrac{-2-7}{3-0} = -\dfrac{9}{3} = -3$	Calculate gradient of median.	
		$y - (-2) = -3(x - 3)$ $y = -3x + 7$ or equivalent	Find equation of median.	
	b)	$m_{AB} = \dfrac{-1-7}{8-0} = -\dfrac{8}{8} = -1$	Calculate gradient of AB.	C
		$m_{AB} \times m_{CE} = -1$		
		$\Rightarrow m_{CE} = 1$	Calculate gradient of CE.	
		$y - (-3) = 1(x - (-2))$		
		$y = x - 1$ or equivalent	Find equation of altitude.	
	c)	e.g. $x - 1 = -3x + 7$		C
		$4x = 8$		
		$x = 2$	Find x- (or y- coordinate)	
		$y = 2 - 1 = 1$	Find y- (or x- coordinate)	
		$(2, 1)$	**8 marks**	

Question			Answer	Marks	Grade demand
58	a)		$M(8, 2)$	Find midpoint of QR.	> C
			$m_{QR} = \dfrac{-4-8}{12-4} = \dfrac{-12}{8} = -\dfrac{3}{2}$	Find gradient of QR.	
			$m_{QR} \times m_{PS} = -1$		
			$\Rightarrow m_{PS} = \dfrac{2}{3}$	Find gradient of PS.	
			$y - 2 = \dfrac{2}{3}(x - 8)$		
			$3y - 6 = 2x - 16$		
			$2x - 3y = 10$ or equivalent	Find equation of PS.	
	b)	i)	e.g. $5x - y = 64$	Start to solve simultaneous equations.	C
			$\quad\quad 2x - 3y = 10$		
			$\quad 15x - 3y = 192$		
			$\underline{-\ \ 2x - 3y = 10}$		
			$\quad 13x \quad\quad = 182$		
			$\quad\quad x \quad\quad = 14$		
			$5 \times 14 - y = 64$		
			$\quad\quad\quad y = 6$		
			$(14, 6)$	Find coordinates of point of intersection.	
		ii)	$\tan\theta = 5$	Use $m = \tan\theta$.	C
			$\theta = 78.7°$ or 1.37 radians	Find size of angle.	
				8 marks	
59	a)		Centre $= (3, -2)$	State coordinates of centre.	C
			$m_{radius} = \dfrac{6 - (-2)}{-1 - 3} = \dfrac{8}{-4} = -2$	Find gradient of radius.	
			$m_{tangent} = \dfrac{1}{2}$	State gradient of tangent.	
			$y - 6 = \dfrac{1}{2}(x - (-1))$		
			$2y - 12 = x + 1$		
			$\Leftrightarrow x - 2y + 13 = 0$ or equivalent	Find equation of tangent.	
	b)		$x^2 + (x - 13)^2 - 6x + 4(x - 13) - 19 = 0$	Substitute $y = x - 13$ into equation of circle.	C
			$2x^2 - 28x + 98 = 0$	Express in standard quadratic form.	
			$2(x - 7)(x - 7) = 0$		
			$x = 7$	Find root.	
			Only one (repeated) root, so line is a tangent to circle.	Conclusion with justification.	
			$x = 7 \Rightarrow y = 7 - 13 = -6$		
			Point of contact is $(7, -6)$.	Find coordinates of points of contact.	
				9 marks	

Question		Answer	Marks	Grade demand
60	a)	$C_1(5,-10)$	Find centre of C_1.	C
		$r_1 = 9$	Find radius of C_1.	
		$C_2(0,2)$	Find centre of C_2.	
		$r_2 = \sqrt{0^2 + (-2)^2 - (-21)} = 5$	Find radius of C_2.	
	b)	$C_1C_2 = \sqrt{(0-5)^2 + (2-(-10))^2} = 13$	Find distance between centres.	> C
		$r_1 + r_2 = 9 + 5 = 14$	Find sum of radii.	
		$14 > 13$, i.e. $r_1 + r_2 > C_1C_2$, so the circles intersect.	State conclusion with justification. **7 marks**	
61		$C_A(-8,-10)$, $r_A = 16$	Find centre and radius of C_A.	> C
		$C_C(16,8)$, $r_C = 6$	Find centre and radius of C_C.	
		$C_AC_C = \sqrt{(16-(-8))^2 + (8-(-10))^2} = 30$	Find distance between centres.	
		$r_B = \frac{1}{2}\left(C_AC_C - (r_1 + r_2)\right)$	Find radius of C_B.	
		$= \frac{1}{2}(30 - (16+6)) = 4$		
		C_B divides C_AC_C in the ratio $2:1$. $x_B = x_A + \frac{2}{3}(x_C - x_A)$	Find ratio in which C_B divides C_AC_C.	
		$= -8 + \frac{2}{3}(16-(-8)) = 8$		
		$y_B = y_A + \frac{2}{3}(y_C - y_A)$		
		$= -10 + \frac{2}{3}(8-(-10)) = 2$		
		$\Rightarrow C_B(8,2)$	Find centre of C_B.	
		$(x-8)^2 + (y-2)^2 = 16$	State equation of C_B. **7 marks**	

Question	Answer	Marks	Grade demand
62	$g^2 + f^2 - c > 0$	Use $g^2 + f^2 - c > 0$.	> C
	$(-k)^2 + (2k)^2 - (-3k+2) > 0$	Identify g, f and c.	
	$5k^2 + 3k - 2 > 0$	Rearrange into standard quadratic form.	
	$(5k - 2)(k + 1) > 0$	Find zeros.	
	Use a table of values or sketch graph of $y = (5k - 2)(k + 1)$ to find correct range of values.	Find correct range of values.	

k		$\rightarrow$	-1	$\rightarrow$	$\dfrac{2}{5}$	$\rightarrow$
$5k^2 + 3k - 2$		$+$	0	$-$	0	$+$

Zeros are $\dfrac{2}{5}$ and -1.

$k < -1$, $k > \dfrac{2}{5}$

5 marks

Paper 1 (non-calculator)

Duration: 1 hour 15 minutes

Total marks: 55

Attempt ALL questions.

You may NOT use a calculator.

Full credit will be given only to solutions which contain appropriate working.

State the units for your answer where appropriate.

Answers obtained by readings from scale drawings will not receive any credit.

MARKS

1 P(-1, 4) and Q(5, -6) are points on the circumference of a circle, as shown in the diagram.

   PQ is a diameter.

   Find the equation of the circle.

   3

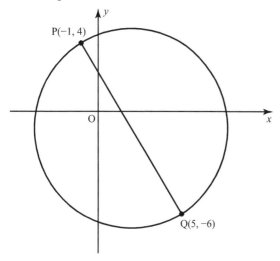

2 A sequence is generated by the recurrence relation $u_{n+1} = au_n + b$, where $-1 < a < 1$ and $u_0 = 40$.

   Given $u_1 = 28$ and $u_2 = 19$, find the values of a and b.

   3

3 Functions $f(x) = \dfrac{1}{x+2}$ and $g(x) = 3x - 4$ are defined on suitable domains.

   a) Find an expression for $h(x)$ where $h(x) = f(g(x))$.

   2

   b) What value of x cannot be in the domain of h?

   1

4 Line AB has equation $\sqrt{3}x + y = 3$ as shown in the diagram.

   The angle between AB and the positive direction of the x-axis is $a°$.

   Calculate the value of a.

   2

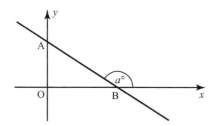

MARKS

5 Given that $f(x) = \dfrac{2x^3 - 1}{x^2}$, find $f'(x)$. 3

6 Find the range of values of k for which $kx^2 - 4x + 3 = 0$ has no real roots. 3

7 Vectors $\mathbf{u} = a\mathbf{i} - 10\mathbf{j} - \mathbf{k}$ and $\mathbf{v} = 2\mathbf{i} + \mathbf{j} - 4\mathbf{k}$ are perpendicular. 2

   Determine the values of a.

8 A sketch of the function $y = f(x)$ is shown in the diagram.

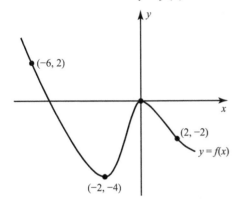

   a) Sketch the graph of $y = f(2x)$. 1

   b) Sketch the graph of $y = 2 - f(2x)$. 2

9 Find algebraically the values of x for which the function $f(x) = x^3 + x^2 - 8x + 3$ is strictly 4
   increasing.

10 Evaluate $\log_4 12 - \left(\log_4 8 + \dfrac{1}{2}\log_4 36 \right)$. 4

11 a) Show that $(x - 2)$ is a factor of $f(x) = 3x^3 - 5x^2 - 4x + 4$. 2

    b) Hence, or otherwise, solve $f(x) = 0$. 3

12 Find $\displaystyle\int \sqrt{2x - 3}\, dx$. 3

13 The diagram shows a right-angled triangle whose sides represent the vectors $\mathbf{a}$, $\mathbf{b}$ 3
    and $\mathbf{c}$.

    The angle between vectors $\mathbf{a}$ and $\mathbf{b}$ is $60°$.

    If $|\mathbf{a}| = 1$ and $|\mathbf{b}| = 2$, evaluate $\mathbf{b}.(\mathbf{a} + \mathbf{c})$.

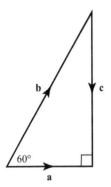

14 a) If $\tan x = \dfrac{1}{4}$, $0 \le x \le \dfrac{\pi}{2}$ find the exact value of $\sin 2x$. 3

    b) Hence find the exact value of $\sin 4x$. 3

15 A piece of land beside a stone wall is to be fenced off with 270 metres of fencing to make two identical rectangular enclosures with sides of length x metres and y metres as shown in the diagram.

The wall provides one boundary, so only three sides of each enclosure need fencing.

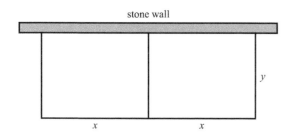

stone wall

a) Show that the combined area of the enclosures is given by $A = 180x - \frac{4}{3}x^2$. **3**

b) Find the maximum area that can be fenced off. **5**

[End of Paper 1]

Paper 2

Duration: 1 hour 30 minutes

Total marks: 65

Attempt ALL questions.

You may use a calculator.

Full credit will be given only to solutions which contain appropriate working.

State the units for your answer where appropriate.

Answers obtained by readings from scale drawings will not receive any credit.

MARKS

1   A triangle PQR has vertices P(−7, 3), Q(9, 5) and R(4, −5) as shown in the diagram.

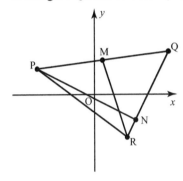

    a)   Find the equation of the median RM.   **3**

    b)   Find the equation of the altitude PN.   **3**

    c)   Find the coordinates of the point of intersection of RM and PN.   **2**

2   Express $2x^2 - 12x + 11$ in the form $a(x+b)^2 + c$.   **3**

3   Find the equation of the tangent to the curve $y = (x-3)^4$ at the point (2, 1).   **3**

4   If $\mathbf{u} = k\begin{pmatrix} 2 \\ 1 \\ -2 \end{pmatrix}$, where $k > 0$ and $\mathbf{u}$ is a unit vector, determine the value of k.   **2**

5   Find the equation of the tangent to the circle $x^2 + y^2 - 6x - 4y + 8 = 0$ at the point (5, 1).   **4**

6   The curve with equation $y = x^3 - x^2 - 6x + 2$ and the line with equation $5x + y - 1 = 0$ are shown in the diagram.

    The curve and the line intersect at the points where $x = -1$ and $x = 1$.

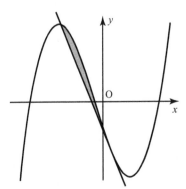

    Find the shaded area enclosed between the line and the curve.   **4**

MARKS

7 ABCD is a quadrilateral with vertices A(−1, 0, −3), B(2, 6, −6), C(8, 9, 6) and D(8, 3, 18) as shown in the diagram.

The point E divides the line AC in the ratio 5 : 4.

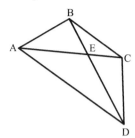

    a) Find the coordinates of E.   2

    b) Calculate the size of the acute angle between the diagonals of quadrilateral ABCD.   4

8 A circle with centre C_1 has equation $(x+5)^2+(y-3)^2=16$.

A second circle with centre C_2 has equation $x^2+y^2-14x+4y+k=0$.

    a) Calculate the distance between the centres of these circles.   3

    b) The two circles intersect.   5

        What is the range of values of k?

9 The mass m_t grams of the radioactive substance radium-226 remaining after t years is given by the formula $m_t=m_0 e^{-0.0004332t}$, where m_0 is the initial mass of the substance.

    a) Given the original mass is 140 grams, find the mass after 100 years.   2

    b) The half-life of any substance is the time taken for the mass to decrease to half of the initial mass.   4

        Find the half-life of radium-226.

10 **a)** Express $15\sin x° + 8\cos x°$ in the form $k\sin(x+a)°$ where $k>0$ and $0\le a\le360$.   4

    b) Hence solve the equation $15\sin x°+8\cos x°=10$ for $0\le x\le360$.   3

11 The rate of change of the height, h metres, of a ball which is thrown vertically upwards is given by $\dfrac{dh}{dt}=20-kt$.   6

    ▶ t is the elapsed time, in seconds, since the ball is thrown.

    ▶ k is a constant.

    ▶ Initially the height of the ball is 2 metres.

    ▶ The ball reaches a height of 15 metres after 1 second.

    Express h in terms of t.

12 Angle ABC = $2x$ and angle CBD = x are shown in the diagram.

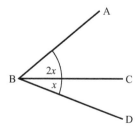

    a) Show that $\cos 3x = 4\cos^3 x - 3\cos x$.   5

    b) Hence find $\int \cos^3 x\, dx$.   3

[End of Practice Paper A]

Paper 1 (non-calculator)

Duration: 1 hour 15 minutes

Total marks: 55

Attempt ALL questions.

You may NOT use a calculator.

Full credit will be given only to solutions which contain appropriate working.

State the units for your answer where appropriate.

Answers obtained by readings from scale drawings will not receive any credit.

MARKS

1. A curve has equation $y = 3x - x^2$. Find the point on the curve where the gradient of the tangent is 4. **4**

2. The function $g(x) = 2 - 3x$ is defined on the set of real numbers.
   Find an expression for $g^{-1}(x)$. **3**

3. PQRS is a parallelogram. P, Q and R have coordinates $(-2, 1)$, $(4, 10)$ and $(6, -5)$.
   Show that the equation of RS is $3x - 2y = 28$. **3**

4. The graph of a function f is shown in the diagram. **3**
   f has a point of inflexion at $(-2, 1)$ and a minimum turning point at $(2, -3)$.
   Sketch the graph of the derived function f'.

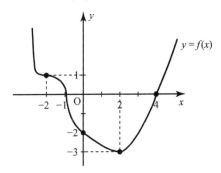

5. Given that $f(x) = 4(5 - 2x)^3$, find $f'(3)$. **3**

6. Find $\int \frac{1}{3} - t^{-2} \, dt$. **4**

7. Solve the equation $\log_5(x - 1) - 3\log_5 2 = 3$. **4**

8 The graph with equation $y = f(x)$ is shown in the diagram.

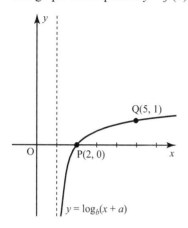

a) Find the values of a and b.   **3**

b) Sketch the graph with equation $y = f^{-1}(x)$.   **2**

9 If x° is an acute angle such that $\cos x^\circ = \dfrac{1}{7}$, show that $\cos(x + 60)^\circ = -\dfrac{11}{14}$.   **5**

10 The points A$(1, -7, -15)$, B$(7, 2, -3)$ and C$(x, 8, 5)$ are collinear.   **2**
Find the value of x.

11 Solve $2\cos 3x - 1 = 0$ for $0 \le x \le \pi$.   **4**

12 The diagram shows a sketch of part of the graph of $y = 4\sin 2x$.   **5**
Find the total shaded area.

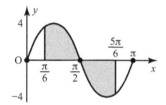

13 For the polynomial $2x^3 + 7x^2 + ax + b$,
▶ $x - 1$ is a factor
▶   20 is the remainder when it is divided by $x + 3$.
Determine the values of a and b.   **4**

14 a) Express $\cos x + \sin x$ in the form $k\cos(x - a)$ where $k > 0$ and $0 \le a \le 2\pi$.   **4**

b) A function, f, is defined by $f(x) = \cos x + \sin x$, $0 < x < 2\pi$.
  (i) State the minimum value of $f(x)$ **1**
  (ii) Determine the value of x where this minimum occurs.   **1**

[End of Paper 1]

Paper 2

Duration: 1 hour 30 minutes

Total marks: 65

Attempt ALL questions.

You may use a calculator.

Full credit will be given only to solutions which contain appropriate working.

State the units for your answer where appropriate.

Answers obtained by readings from scale drawings will not receive any credit.

MARKS

1 Functions $f(x) = \dfrac{1}{x+3}$ and $g(x) = \dfrac{1}{x} - 3$ are defined on suitable domains.

   a) Find an expression for $f(g(x))$. **3**

       Give your answer in its simplest form.

   b) What is the connection between the functions f and g? **1**

2 VPQRS is a pyramid with rectangular base PQRS. **3**

   T is the midpoint of QR.

   Relative to some appropriate axes,

   $\overrightarrow{PQ}$ represents $5\mathbf{i} + 5\mathbf{j} - 5\mathbf{k}$

   $\overrightarrow{PS}$ represents $4\mathbf{i} + 4\mathbf{j} + 8\mathbf{k}$

   $\overrightarrow{PV}$ represents $6\mathbf{i} + 11\mathbf{j} + 9\mathbf{k}$

   Find $\overrightarrow{VT}$ in component form.

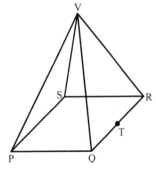

3 Two circles, with centres A and B, have equations $x^2 + y^2 - 4x - 60 = 0$ and
$x^2 + y^2 - 20x - 30y + 300 = 0$, respectively.

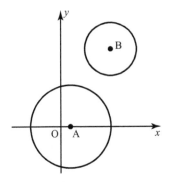

   a) Find the distance between the centres of the two circles. **3**

b) Hence, calculate the size of the smallest gap between the two circles as shown in the diagram.

3

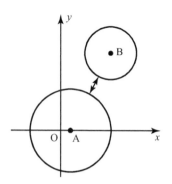

4 OABCD is a pyramid.

A is the point (24, 0, 0), B is (24, 16, 0) and D is (12, 8, 20).
E divides DB in the ratio 3 : 1.

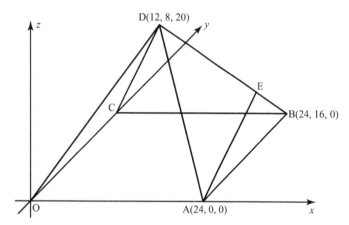

a) Find the coordinates of the point E.

2

b) Calculate the components of $\overrightarrow{AD}$ and $\overrightarrow{AE}$.

2

c) Calculate the size of angle DAE.

4

5 A chord joins the points P(−2, 0) and Q(3, 5) on a circle as shown in the diagram.

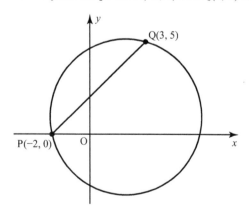

a) Show that the equation of the perpendicular bisector of chord PQ is $x + y = 3$.

4

MARKS

b) The point C is the centre of the circle and RQ is the diameter with equation $y = 4x - 7$.

Find the coordinates of the point C.

2

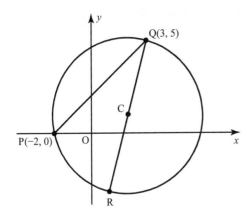

c) Find the equation of the circle.

2

6 Rory puts £2100 into a bank account on the first of each month.

He spends 96% of the amount in the account by the end of the month. The account earns no interest.

a) **(i)** Write down a recurrence relation for the amount of money, A_n, in his account on the first day of the nth month.

2

(ii) How much will be in the account in the long term on the first of each month?

1

b) Rory wants to have £2400 in the account in the long term on the first of each month.

What percentage of the money in the account should he spend each month?

3

7 A curve with equation $y = f(x)$ passes through the point $(2, -1)$ and is such that $f'(x) = 3 - \dfrac{4}{x^2}$. Express $f(x)$ in terms of x.

4

8 The population of a city t years after 2015 can be approximated by the formula $P = 243\,500e^{0.008t}$.

a) Find the population of the city in the year 2015.

1

b) How many years would it take for the population of the city to reach $330\,000$?

4

9 The equation $x^2 + x(1 - k) + 1 - k = 0$ has two real and distinct roots.

Determine the range of values for k.

4

10 Find the x-coordinates of the stationary points on the graph with equation $y = f(x)$, where $f(x) = x^3 + x^2 - x - 2$.

4

11 Two variables, x and y, are related by the equation $y = be^{ax}$.

If $\log_e y$ is plotted against x, the following graph is obtained.
Find the values of a and b.

4

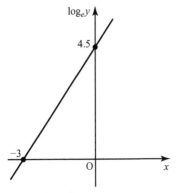

12 Acceleration is defined as the rate of change of velocity. An object is travelling in a straight line.

Its velocity, v m s^{-1}, t seconds after the start of its motion, is given by $v(t) = 1 + 5t - t^2$.

   a) Find a formula for $a(t)$, the acceleration of this object, t seconds after the start of its motion.   **2**

   b) Velocity is defined as the rate of change of displacement.   **3**

        Find a formula for $s(t)$, the displacement of the object, given that $s(t) = 2$ when $t = 0$.

13 Solve $\cos 2\theta + \cos \theta = 0$ for $0 \leq \theta < 2\pi$.   **4**

[End of Practice Paper B]

Practice Paper A

Paper 1 (non-calculator)

Question		Answer	Marks	Commentary, hints and tips	Grade demand
1		$C = \left(\dfrac{-1+5}{2}, \dfrac{4+(-6)}{2}\right)$ $= (2, -1)$ $r^2 = CP^2 = (2-(-1))^2 + (-1-4)^2$ $= 3^2 + (-5)^2$ $= 34$ $(x-2)^2 + (y+1)^2 = 34$	Find centre. Find the square of the radius. State equation of circle. **3 marks**	C is the midpoint of PQ. CP (or CQ) is a radius.	C
2	a)	$28 = 40a + b$ $19 = 28a + b$ $12a + 9$ $a = \dfrac{3}{4}$ $28 = 40 \times \dfrac{3}{4} + b$ $28 = 30 + b$ $b = -2$	Form equation connecting u_0 and u_1. Form equation connecting u_1 and u_2. Find value of a and b. **3 marks**	Substitute $u_1 = 28$, $u_0 = 40$ into $u_1 = au_0 + b$. and $u_1 = 19$, $u_0 = 28$ into $u_2 = au_1 + b$.	C
3	a)	$f(3x-4) = \dfrac{1}{(3x-4)+2}$ $= \dfrac{1}{3x-2}$	Start composite process. Find $h(x)$ in simplest form. State value.	$f(g(x)) = \dfrac{1}{g(x)+2}$	C
	b)	$x = \dfrac{2}{3}$	**3 marks**		C
4		$\sqrt{3}x + y = 3$ $\Leftrightarrow y = -\sqrt{3}x + 3$ $\Rightarrow m = -\sqrt{3}$ $\Rightarrow \tan a° = -\sqrt{3}$ $a = 120$	Use $m = \tan a°$. Calculate angle. **2 marks**	Rearrange the equation into the form $y = mx + c$ in order to find the gradient then use $m = \tan a°$.	C

Question	Answer	Marks	Commentary, hints and tips	Grade demand
5	$f(x) = 2x - x^{-2}$	Prepare to differentiate.	Rearrange $f(x)$ into the form $ax^n + bx^m$ before differentiating, i.e. $\dfrac{2x^3 - 1}{x^2} = \dfrac{2x^3}{x^2} - \dfrac{1}{x^2} = 2x - x^{-2}$	C
	$f'(x) = 2 \ldots$	Differentiate first term.		
	$= 2 + 2x^{-3}$	Differentiate second term. **3 marks**		
6	$b^2 - 4ac < 0$	Use discriminant < 0.	No real roots so $b^2 - 4ac < 0$.	C
	$a = k,\ b = -4,\ c = 3$	Identify a, b and c.		
	$16 - 12k < 0$			
	$k > \dfrac{4}{3}$	Find range of values of k in simplest form. **3 marks**		
7	$2a - 10 + 4 = 0$ $a = 3$	Equate scalar product to zero. Find value of a. **2 marks**	$\mathbf{u}$, $\mathbf{v}$ perpendicular $\Leftrightarrow$ $\mathbf{u}.\mathbf{v} = 0$	C
8 a)		Compress horizontally by a factor of 2 with all points correctly annotated.	$f(x) \to f(2x)$ $\Rightarrow (x, y) \to \left(\dfrac{x}{2}, y\right)$ e.g. $(-6, 2) \to (-3, 2)$	C
b)		Reflect $y = f(2x)$ in x-axis. Then vertical translation of 2 units up with all points correctly annotated. **3 marks**	$2 - f(2x) = -f(2x) + 2$ $f(2x) \to -f(2x) \to -f(2x) + 2$ $\Rightarrow \left(\dfrac{x}{2}, y\right) \to \left(\dfrac{x}{2}, -y\right) \to \left(\dfrac{x}{2}, -y+2\right)$ e.g. $(-3, 2) \to (-3, -2) \to (-3, 0)$	C

Question	Answer	Marks	Commentary, hints and tips	Grade demand
9	$f'(x) = 3x^2 + 2x - 8$	Differentiate.		C
	$3x^2 + 2x - 8 > 0$ $(3x-4)(x+2) > 0$	Set derivative greater than 0.	$f(x)$ is increasing when $f'(x) > 0$.	
	Zeros are $\frac{4}{3}$ and -2	Find zeros.	Use a table of values or a sketch graph of $y = (3x-4)(x+2)$ to solve $(3x-4)(x+2) > 0$.	
	<table><tr><td>x</td><td>$\to$</td><td>-2</td><td>$\to$</td><td>$\frac{4}{3}$</td><td>$\frac{4}{3}$</td></tr><tr><td>$f'(x)$</td><td>$+$</td><td>0</td><td>$-$</td><td>0</td><td>$+$</td></tr></table>			
	$x < -2, x > \frac{4}{3}$	Find correct range of values with justification. **4 marks**		
10	$\log_4 12 - (\log_4 8 + \log_4 36^{\frac{1}{2}})$	Use $n\log_a x = \log_a x^n$.	Use the laws of logarithms to simplify the expression into the form $\log_4 a$.	C
	$= \log_4 12 - (\log_4 8 + \log_4 6)$			
	$= \log_4 12 - \log_4(8 \times 6)$	Use $\log_a x + \log_a y = \log_a xy$.		
	$= \log_4 12 - \log_4 48$			
	$= \log_4 \frac{12}{48}$	Use $\log_a x - \log_a y = \log_a \frac{x}{y}$.		
	$= \log_4 \frac{1}{4}$	Evaluate.	$\log_4 \frac{1}{4} = \log_4 4^{-1} = -1$	
	$= -1$	**4 marks**		
11			Use synthetic division to show that has $f(x) \div (x-2)$ has remainder 0.	C
a)	<table><tr><td>2</td><td>3</td><td>-5</td><td>-4</td><td>4</td></tr><tr><td></td><td></td><td></td><td></td><td></td></tr><tr><td></td><td>3</td><td></td><td></td><td></td></tr></table>	Know to use $x = 2$ in synthetic division table		
	<table><tr><td>2</td><td>3</td><td>-5</td><td>-4</td><td>4</td></tr><tr><td></td><td></td><td>6</td><td>2</td><td>-4</td></tr><tr><td></td><td>3</td><td>1</td><td>-2</td><td>0</td></tr></table>		Remember to state conclusion with justification.	
	Remainder $= 0 \therefore (x-2)$ is a factor	Complete division, interpret result and state conclusion		
b)	$(x-2)(3x^2 + x - 2) = 0$	State quadratic factor		C
	$(x-2)(3x-2)(x+1) = 0$	Find remaining factors		
	$x = 1, \frac{2}{3}, 2$	Find solution		
		5 marks		

Question	Answer	Marks	Commentary, hints and tips	Grade demand
12	$\int (2x-3)^{\frac{1}{2}}\,dx$	Prepare to integrate.	Express the integral in the form $\int (ax+b)^n\,dx$ before integrating.	> C
	$=\dfrac{(2x-3)^{\frac{3}{2}}}{\frac{3}{2}}\cdots$	Start to integrate.	$\int (ax+b)^n\,dx = \dfrac{(ax+b)^{n+1}}{a(n+1)} + c$	
	$=\dfrac{(2x-3)^{\frac{3}{2}}}{\frac{3}{2}\times 2}\cdots$			
	$=\dfrac{(2x-3)^{\frac{3}{2}}}{3}+c$	Complete integration. **3 marks**	Remember to add c, the constant of integration.	
13	**Method 1** $\mathbf{b}.(\mathbf{a}+\mathbf{c}) = \mathbf{b}.\mathbf{a}+\mathbf{b}.\mathbf{c}$ $\mathbf{b}.\mathbf{a} = 2\times 1\times \cos 60$ $\mathbf{b}.\mathbf{c} = 2\times\sqrt{3}\times \cos 150$ $\mathbf{b}.(\mathbf{a}+\mathbf{c}) = 1-3 = -2$ **Method 2**	**Method 1** Expand brackets. Start to evaluate $\mathbf{b}.\mathbf{a}$ and $\mathbf{b}.\mathbf{c}$. Evaluate $\mathbf{b}.(\mathbf{a}+\mathbf{c})$. **Method 2** Interpret pathway for $\mathbf{a}+\mathbf{c}$.	Expand the brackets and then use $\mathbf{b}.\mathbf{a} = \|\mathbf{b}\|\|\mathbf{a}\|\cos\theta$ and $\mathbf{b}.\mathbf{c} = \|\mathbf{b}\|\|\mathbf{c}\|\cos\theta$.	> C
	  $\mathbf{b}.(\mathbf{a}+\mathbf{c}) = 2\times 2\times \cos 120$ $=-2$	Start to evaluate $\mathbf{b}.(\mathbf{a}+\mathbf{c})$. Evaluate $\mathbf{b}.(\mathbf{a}+\mathbf{c})$. **3 marks**		

Question		Answer	Marks	Commentary, hints and tips	Grade demand
14	a)	$2\sin x \cos x$	Use double angle formula.	Use $\sin 2x = 2\sin x \cos x$.	C
		$= 2 \times \dfrac{1}{\sqrt{17}} \times \dfrac{4}{\sqrt{17}}$	Substitute exact values of $\sin x$ and $\cos x$.	Use $\tan x = \dfrac{1}{4} = \dfrac{\text{opposite}}{\text{adjacent}}$ and Pythagoras' theorem to sketch an appropriate right-angled triangle and hence deduce the values of $\sin x$ and $\cos x$.	
		$= \dfrac{8}{17}$	Find exact value of $\sin 2x$.		
	b)	$2\sin 2x \cos 2x$	Use double angle formula.	Use $\sin(2(2x)) = 2\sin 2x \cos 2x$.	> C
		$= 2 \times \dfrac{8}{17} \times \dfrac{15}{17}$	Substitute exact values of $\sin 2x$ and $\cos 2x$.	Use $\sin 2x = \dfrac{8}{17} = \dfrac{\text{opposite}}{\text{hypotenuse}}$ and Pythagoras' theorem to sketch an appropriate right-angled triangle and hence deduce the value of $\cos 2x$.	
		$= \dfrac{240}{289}$	Find exact value of $\sin 4x$.		
			6 marks		
15	a)	$2x + 3y = 270$	Form equation for length of fencing.	Area = length × breadth = $2xy$, but in order to obtain an expression in terms of only x, set up an equation modelling the total length of fencing. Use this equation to express y in terms of x and substitute for y in $A = 2xy$.	> C
		$y = 90 - \dfrac{2}{3}x$	Change subject to y.		
		$A = 2xy$	Show steps leading to given formula for area.		
		$= 2x\left(90 - \dfrac{2x}{3}\right)$			
		$= 180x - \dfrac{4}{3}x^2$			
	b)	$\dfrac{dA}{dx} = 180 - \dfrac{8}{3}x$	Differentiate.		> C
		$180 - \dfrac{8}{3}x = 0$ at S.P.	Set derivative equal to zero.	At stationary points $\dfrac{dA}{dx} = 0$.	
		$x = 67 \cdot 5$	Solve for x.		
		(see table below)	Justify nature of stationary point.	Alternatively, $\dfrac{d^2A}{dx^2}$ may be used to justify the nature of stationary point as follows: $\dfrac{d^2A}{dx^2} = -\dfrac{8}{3}$, hence a maximum since $\dfrac{d^2A}{dx^2} < 0$.	
		$y = 90 - \dfrac{2}{3} \times 67 \cdot 5 = 45$	Find maximum area.		
		$A = 2 \times 67 \cdot 5 \times 45 = 6075\,\text{m}^2$	**8 marks**		

x	←	67.5	→
$\dfrac{dA}{dx}$	+	0	−
slope	/	―	\

Hence $x = 67.5$ gives a maximum value for the area

Paper 2

Question		Answer	Marks	Commentary, hints and tips	Grade demand
1	a)	$M = (1, 4)$	Calculate midpoint of PQ.	Median RM is a line from R to the midpoint of PQ.	C
		$m_{RM} = -3$	Calculate gradient of median.	Simplify the equation.	
		$y + 5 = -3(x - 4)$		(Any equivalent simplified version is acceptable.)	
		$3x + y = 7$	Find equation of median.		
	b)	$m_{QR} = 2$	Calculate gradient of QR.	Altitude PN is perpendicular to QR, hence $m_{PN} \times m_{QR} = -1$.	C
		$m_{PN} = -\dfrac{1}{2}$	Calculate gradient of PN.		
		$y - 3 = -\dfrac{1}{2}(x - (-7))$		Simplify the equation.	
		$x + 2y = -1$	Find equation of altitude.	(Any equivalent simplified version is acceptable.)	
	c)	e.g. $3x + y = 7$		Use simultaneous equations to find where the two lines intersect.	C
		$x + 2y = -1$			
		so $6x + 2y = 14$			
		$x + 2y = -1$			
		so $x = 3$ (or $y = -2$)	Find x- (or y- coordinate)		
		$(3, -2)$	Find y- (or x- coordinate)		
			8 marks		
2		$2(x^2 - 6x) + 11$	Use common factor.	Complete square for $2(x^2 - 6x)$ first, then add the 11 at the end.	C
		$2((x - 3)^2 - 9) + 11$	Start to complete square.		
		$2(x - 3)^2 - 18 + 11$	Complete process.		
		$2(x - 3)^2 - 7$	**3 marks**		
3		$\dfrac{dy}{dx} = 4(x - 3)^3$	Differentiate.	The gradient of the tangent is the value of $\dfrac{dy}{dx}$ when $x = 2$.	C
		$x = 2, \dfrac{dy}{dx} = 4(2 - 3)^3$			
		$= -4$	Evaluate derivative.		
		$y - 1 = -4(x - 2)$	Find equation of tangent.	Simplify the equation.	
		$\Leftrightarrow y = -4x + 9$	**3 marks**	(Any equivalent simplified version is acceptable.)	
4		$\|\mathbf{u}\| = \sqrt{2^2 + 1^2 + (-2^2)} = 3$	Find $\|\mathbf{u}\|$	The magnitude of a unit vector is 1.	C
		$k = \dfrac{1}{3}$	Find k		
			2 marks		
5		centre $= (3, 2)$	Find coordinates of centre of circle.		C
		$m_{radius} = \dfrac{1 - 2}{5 - 3} = -\dfrac{1}{2}$	Find gradient of radius.	The tangent is the line through $(5, 1)$ which is perpendicular to the radius.	
		$m_{tangent} = 2$	Find gradient of tangent.	The tangent is perpendicular to radius hence $m_{tangent} \times m_{radius} = -1$.	
		$y - 1 = 2(x - 5)$		Simplify the equation.	
		$\Leftrightarrow y - 1 = 2x - 10$		(Any equivalent simplified version is acceptable.)	
		$\Leftrightarrow y = 2x - 9$	Find equation of tangent.		
			4 marks		

Question		Answer	Marks	Commentary, hints and tips	Grade demand
6		$\int_{-1}^{1}(x^3 - x^2 - 6x + 2$ $\qquad -(-5x+1))dx$ $= \int_{-1}^{1}(x^3 - x^2 - x + 1)\,dx$	State integral	Upper − lower = equation of the curve − equation of the line. Simplify expression for upper − lower before integrating.	C
		$\left[\dfrac{x^4}{4} - \dfrac{x^3}{3} - \dfrac{x^2}{2} + x\right]_{-1}^{1}$	Integrate.		
		$= \left(\dfrac{1}{4} - \dfrac{1}{3} - \dfrac{1}{2} + 1\right)$ $\qquad -\left(\dfrac{1}{4} + \dfrac{1}{3} - \dfrac{1}{2} - 1\right)$	Substitute limits.	$= \dfrac{1}{4} - \dfrac{1}{4} - \dfrac{1}{3} - \dfrac{1}{3} - \dfrac{1}{2} + \dfrac{1}{2} + 1 + 1$ $= -\dfrac{2}{3} + 2 = 1\dfrac{1}{3}$	
		$= 1\dfrac{1}{3}$ units^2	Evaluate area. **4 marks**		
7	a)	$\overrightarrow{AE} = \dfrac{5}{9}\overrightarrow{AC}$	Interpret ratio.		C
		$\Rightarrow \mathbf{e} - \mathbf{a} = \dfrac{5}{9}(\mathbf{c} - \mathbf{a})$			
		$\Rightarrow \mathbf{e} = \dfrac{1}{9}(5\mathbf{c} + 4\mathbf{a})$			
		$\mathbf{e} = \dfrac{1}{9}\left(\begin{pmatrix} 40 \\ 45 \\ 30 \end{pmatrix} + \begin{pmatrix} -4 \\ 0 \\ -12 \end{pmatrix}\right)$			
		$\Rightarrow E\,(4,5,2)$	Find coordinates of E.	Remember to give the final answer as coordinates **not** components.	
	b)	$\overrightarrow{EA}.\overrightarrow{EB} = 45$	Evaluate $\overrightarrow{EA}.\overrightarrow{EB}$	Use vectors that **both** point away from (or towards) the vertex of the angle.	
		$\left|\overrightarrow{EA}\right| = \sqrt{75}$ and $\left|\overrightarrow{EB}\right| = \sqrt{69}$	Evaluate $\left|\overrightarrow{EA}\right|$ and $\left|\overrightarrow{EB}\right|$	Don't approximate values of surds, e.g. $\sqrt{75} = 8.7$.	
		$\cos AEB = \dfrac{45}{\sqrt{75}\sqrt{69}}$	Use scalar product Calculate angle	Premature rounding may lead to an incorrect final answer.	
		angle $AEB = 51.3^\circ$	**7 marks**		
8	a)	centre $C_1 = (-5, 3)$	Find centre of C_1.		C
		centre $C_2 = (7, -2)$	Find centre of C_2.		
		$C_1C_2 = \sqrt{(7-(-5))^2 + (-2-3)^2}$ $\qquad = 13$	Find distance between centres.		

Question		Answer	Marks	Commentary, hints and tips	Grade demand
8	b)	radius $C_1 = 4$ radius $C_2 = \sqrt{53-k}$ $k < 53$ $4 + \sqrt{53-k} > 13$ $\sqrt{53-k} > 9$ $53 - k > 81$ $k < -28$	Find radius of first circle. Find radius of second circle in terms of k. Find upper bound for k. Use $r_1 + r_2 > C_1C_2$. Find lower bound for k. **8 marks**	Two circles do not intersect if the sum of their radii is greater than the distance between their centres.	$> C$
9	a)	$m_{100} = 140 \times e^{-0.0004332 \times 100}$ $= 134$ grams	Substitute for m_0 and t in formula. Evaluate formula.		C
	b)	$\frac{1}{2} m_0 = m_0 e^{-0.0004332t}$ $e^{-0.0004332t} = \frac{1}{2}$ $-0.0004332t = \ln\left(\frac{1}{2}\right)$ $t = \dfrac{\ln\left(\frac{1}{2}\right)}{-0.0004332}$ $= 1600$ years	Interpret half-life. Process equation. Write in logarithmic form. Solve to find half-life. **6 marks**	The half-life is the time for which $m_t = \frac{1}{2}m_0$. Remember $e^x = y \Leftrightarrow x = \ln y$. Don't approximate the value of $\ln\left(\frac{1}{2}\right)$. Premature rounding may lead to an incorrect final answer.	$> C$
10	a)	$15\sin x + 8\cos x =$ $k(\sin x \cos a + \cos x \sin a)$ $k\cos a = 15, k\sin a = 8$ $k = \sqrt{15^2 + 8^2} = 17$ $a = \tan^{-1}\left(\frac{8}{15}\right) = 28$ $15\sin x + 8\cos x = 17\sin(x + 28)$	Use addition formula. Equate coefficients. Find k. Find a and state expression in required form.	Use the expansion for $\sin(A + B)$ from the Formulae list.	C
	b)	$17\sin(x + 28) = 10$ $\sin(x + 28) = \frac{10}{17}$ $x + 28 = 36, 144$ $x = 8, 116$	Equate wave function with 10. Solve for $x + 28$. Solve for x. **7 marks**	link to part (a).. $\sin(x + 28)$ is positive so there are solutions in the 1st and 2nd quadrants.	$> C$

Question		Answer	Marks	Commentary, hints and tips	Grade demand
11		$h = \int (20 - kt)\, dt$	Know to integrate.	Integrate $\dfrac{dh}{dt}$ to obtain h, since integration is the inverse of differentiation.	> C
		$= 20t \ldots\ldots$	Integrate first term.		
		$= 20t - \dfrac{kt^2}{2} + \ldots$	Integrate second term.		
		$= 20t - \dfrac{kt^2}{2} + c$		Remember to add c, the constant of integration.	
		$20 \times 0 - \dfrac{k \times 0^2}{2} + c = 2$		Substitute $h = 24$ and $t = 0$ into the result of the integration to find the value of c.	
		$\Rightarrow c = 2$	Find constant of integration.		
		$20 \times 1 - \dfrac{k \times 1^2}{2} + 2 = 15$	Find value of k.		
		$\Rightarrow \dfrac{1}{2}k = 7$			
		$\Rightarrow k = 14$			
		$h = 20t - 7t^2 + 2$	Express h in terms of t.		
			6 marks		
12	a)	$\cos ABD = \cos(2x + x)$	Use $ABD = \cos(2x + x)$.	The diagram shows that angle $ABD = 2x + x$, so $\cos ABD = \cos(2x + x)$.	> C
		$= \cos 2x \cos x - \sin 2x \sin x$	Use addition formula.	Use the expansions for $\cos(A + B)$ and $\cos 2A$ from the Formulae list.	
		$= (2\cos^2 x - 1)\cos x -$ $(2 \sin x \cos x) \sin x$	Use double angle formulae.		
		$= 2\cos^3 x - \cos x - 2\sin^2 x \cos x$	Expand brackets and use $\sin^2 x = 1 - \cos^2 x$.	Use $\sin^2 x = 1 - \cos^2 x$ from the National 5 course.	
		$= 2\cos^3 x - \cos x - 2(1 - \cos^2 x)\cos x$	Expand brackets and rearrange into required form.	Since the answer is given, show **all** the steps leading to it.	
		$= 2\cos^3 x - \cos 2x - 2\cos x + 2\cos^3 x$			
		$= 4\cos^3 x - 3\cos x$			
	b)	$\dfrac{1}{4} \int (\cos 3x + 3\cos x)\, dx$	Use $\cos^3 x = \dfrac{1}{4}(\cos 3x + 3\cos x)$.	Make $\cos^3 x$ the subject of the answer to part a). Hence rewrite the integral in a form that can be integrated.	> C
		$= \dfrac{1}{4}\left(\dfrac{1}{3}\sin 3x + \ldots \right)$	Integrate first term.	Remember to add c, the constant of integration.	
		$= \dfrac{1}{4}\left(\dfrac{1}{3}\sin 3x + 3\sin x \right) + c$	Complete integration.		
			8 marks		

Practice Paper B

Paper 1 (non-calculator)

Question	Answer	Marks	Commentary, hints and tips	Grade demand
1	$\dfrac{dy}{dx} = 3 - 2x$	Differentiate.		C
	$3 - 2x = 4$	Set derivative equal to 4.	The gradient of the tangent is 4	
		Solve equation.	$\Rightarrow \dfrac{dy}{dx} = 4.$	
	$x = -\dfrac{1}{2}$			
	$y = 3 \times \left(-\dfrac{1}{2}\right) - \left(-\dfrac{1}{2}\right)^2 = -\dfrac{7}{4}$			
	$\left(-\dfrac{1}{2}, -\dfrac{7}{4}\right)$	State coordinates of point.		
		4 marks		
2	$y = 2 - 3x$	Substitute y for $g(x)$ and start to rearrange.	Start by changing the subject of	C
	$3x + y = 2$		$y = \dfrac{1}{2 - x}$ to x.	
	$3x = 2 - y$			
	$x = \dfrac{2 - y}{3}$	Complete rearrangement.		
	$g^{-1}(x) = \dfrac{2 - x}{3}$	State inverse function.	Remember to express $g^{-1}(x)$ in terms of x.	
		3 marks		
3	$m_{PQ} = \dfrac{10 - 1}{4 - (-2)} = \dfrac{9}{6} = \dfrac{3}{2}$	Find gradient of PQ.	Opposite sides of a parallelogram are parallel and therefore have the same gradient.	C
	$\Rightarrow m_{RS} = \dfrac{3}{2}$		Since the answer is given, show all steps leading to the required answer.	
	$y - (-5) = \dfrac{3}{2}(x - 6)$	Start to find equation of RS.		
	$2y + 10 = 3x - 18$	Find equation of RS in required form.		
	$3x - 2y = 28$			
		3 marks		
4		Roots at -2 and 2. Turning point at $(-2, 0)$. Correct shape.	Stationary points of $f(x)$ are roots of $f'(x)$. The graph of $f'(x)$ is above the x-axis where the gradient of $f(x)$ is positive and below the x-axis where the gradient of $f(x)$ is negative.	> C
		3 marks		
5	$f'(x) = 12(5 - 2x)^2 \ldots\ldots$	Start to differentiate.	Use the chain rule.	C
	$= -24(5 - 2x)^2$	Complete differentiation.		
	$f'(3) = -24(5 - 2 \times 3)^2$	Evaluate $f'(3)$.		
	$= -24$	**3 marks**		

Question		Answer	Marks	Commentary, hints and tips	Grade demand
6		$\int \dfrac{1}{3} - t^{-2}\, dt$	Prepare to integrate	Rewrite the integral in the form $a - bt^n$ before integrating, i.e.	C
		$\dfrac{1}{3}t$	Integrate first term	$\dfrac{t^2 - 3}{3t^2} = \dfrac{t^2}{3t^2} - \dfrac{3}{3t^2}$	
		$\cdots \dfrac{t^{-1}}{-1}$	Integrate second term	$= \dfrac{1}{3} - \dfrac{1}{t^2} = \dfrac{1}{3} - t^{-2}$	
		$\dfrac{1}{3}t + t^{-1} + c$	Complete integration and simplify		
			4 marks		
7		$\log_5(x-1) - \log_5 2^3 = 3$	Use $n\log_a x = \log_a x^n$.	Use the laws of logarithms to express the equation in the form $\log_5 f(x) = 3$ then convert into exponential form and solve the resulting equation.	C
		$\log_5(x-1) - \log_5 8 = 3$	Use $\log_a x - \log_a y = \log_a \dfrac{x}{y}$.		
		$\log_5\left(\dfrac{x-1}{8}\right) = 3$			
		$\dfrac{x-1}{8} = 5^3$	Convert to exponential form.		
		$\dfrac{x-1}{8} = 125$			
		$x - 1 = 1000$	Solve for x.		
		$x = 1001$	**4 marks**		
8	a)	**Method 1**	**Method 1**	Use the graph of $f(x) = \log_a x$.	C
		$\log_b x$ cuts x-axis at $(1, 0)$ hence $\log_b x \to a = \log_b(x+a)$ under horizontal translation of 1 unit right	Identify relevant facts.		
		$a = -1$	State value of a.		
		$b = 4$	State value of b.		
		Method 2	**Method 2**	Substitute $(2, 0)$ into $y = \log_b(x+a)$ and solve to obtain a, then substitute value of a and $(5, 1)$ into $y = \log_b(x+a)$ and solve to obtain b.	
		$y = \log_b(x+a)$	Substitute $(2, 0)$ into $y = \log_b(x+a)$.		
		$\log_b(2+a) = 0$			
		$2 + a = b^0 = 1$			
		So $a = -1$	Find value of a.		
		$4 = b^1$ so $b = 4$	Find value of b.		
	b)		Reflect in the line $y = x$ with one point correctly annotated.	The graph contains no points with x coordinate ≤ 1.	C
			Second point correctly annotated and image asymptote shown.	$f(x) \to f^{-1}(x)$ $\Rightarrow (x, y) \to (y, x)$ e.g. $(2,0) \to (0,2)$ and $x = 1 \to y = 1$	
			6 marks		

Question	Answer	Marks	Commentary, hints and tips	Grade demand
9	$\cos x \cos 60 - \sin x \sin 60$ $= \cos x \times \dfrac{1}{2} - \sin x \times \dfrac{\sqrt{3}}{2}$ $= \dfrac{1}{7} \times \dfrac{1}{2} - \dfrac{\sqrt{48}}{7} \times \dfrac{\sqrt{3}}{2}$ $= \dfrac{1}{14} - \dfrac{4\sqrt{3}}{7} \times \dfrac{\sqrt{3}}{2}$ $= \dfrac{1}{14} - \dfrac{12}{14}$ $= -\dfrac{11}{14}$	Use addition formula. Substitute exact values of $\cos 60$ and $\sin 60$ into expansion. Substitute exact values of $\cos x$ and $\sin x$ into expansion. Simplify $\sqrt{48}$. Complete proof. **5 marks**	Use the formula for $\cos(A+B)$ from the Formulae list. Use $\cos x = \dfrac{1}{7} = \dfrac{\text{adjacent}}{\text{hypotenuse}}$ and Pythagoras' theorem to sketch an appropriate right-angled triangle and hence deduce the value of $\sin x$. Use the exact values of $\cos 60$ and $\sin 60$.	C
10	$\overrightarrow{AB} = \begin{pmatrix} 6 \\ 9 \\ 12 \end{pmatrix}$, $\overrightarrow{BC} = \begin{pmatrix} x-7 \\ 6 \\ 8 \end{pmatrix}$ $\Rightarrow \overrightarrow{BC} = \dfrac{2}{3}\overrightarrow{AB}$ $\Rightarrow x - 7 = 4$ $\Rightarrow x = 11$	Find k such that $\overrightarrow{BC} = k\overrightarrow{AB}$. Find value of x. **2 marks**	If A, B and C are collinear then $\overrightarrow{BC} = k\overrightarrow{AB}$. Use the components of $\overrightarrow{AB}$ and $\overrightarrow{BC}$ to obtain the value of k.	> C
11	$\cos 3x = \dfrac{1}{2}$ $3x = \dfrac{\pi}{3}, \dfrac{5\pi}{3}\ldots$ $3x = \ldots \dfrac{7\pi}{3}$ $x = \dfrac{\pi}{9}, \dfrac{5\pi}{9}, \dfrac{7\pi}{9}$	Rearrange equation. Solve for $0 \le 3x \le \pi$. Solve for $\pi \le 3x \le 3\pi$. Solve for $0 \le x \le \pi$. **4 marks**	Because of the multiple angle, $3x$, find all the solutions in the interval $0 \le 3x \le 3\pi$.	> C

Question		Answer	Marks	Commentary, hints and tips	Grade demand
12		$\int_{\frac{\pi}{6}}^{\frac{\pi}{2}} 4\sin 2x\,dx$	Correct integral for area above x-axis	Calculate the areas above and below the x-axis separately then add them together.	> C
		$= [-2\cos 2x]_{\frac{\pi}{6}}^{\frac{\pi}{2}}$	Integrate		
		$= -2\left(\cos\pi - \cos\frac{\pi}{3}\right)$	Substitute limits		
		$= -2\left(-1 - \frac{1}{2}\right)$	Evaluate integral		
		$= 3$		From the symmetry of the graph the shaded areas above and below the x-axis are equal.	
		Total area $= 3 + 3 = 6$ units^2	Evaluate total area **5 marks**		
13		$\begin{array}{r|rrrr} 1 & 2 & 7 & a & b \\ & & 2 & 9 & a+9 \\ \hline & 2 & 9 & a+9 & a+b+9=0 \end{array}$	Use $x = 1$ to obtain equation.	Use synthetic division to obtain a pair of simultaneous equations.	> C
		$\begin{array}{r|rrrr} -3 & 2 & 7 & a & b \\ & & -6 & -3 & -3a+9 \\ \hline & 2 & 1 & a-3 & -3a+b+9=20 \end{array}$	Use $x = -3$ to obtain equation.		
		$\begin{aligned} a+b &= -9 \\ -\quad -3a+b &= 11 \\ \hline 4a &= -20 \end{aligned}$	Use simultaneous equations.		
		$a = -5, b = -4$	Find a and b. **4 marks**		
14	a)	$\cos x + \sin x =$ $k(\cos x^\circ \cos a^\circ + \sin x^\circ \sin a^\circ)$	Use addition formula.	Use expansion for $\cos(A-B)$ from the Formulae list.	C
		$k\cos a = 1,\ k\sin a = 1$	Equate coefficients.		
		$k = \sqrt{1^2 + 1^2} = \sqrt{2}$	Find k.		
		$a = \tan^{-1}\left(\frac{1}{1}\right) = \frac{\pi}{4}$	Find a and state expression in required form.		
		$\cos x - \sin x = \sqrt{2}\cos\left(x - \frac{\pi}{4}\right)$			
	b)	Min value $= \sqrt{2} \times -1 = -\sqrt{2}$	State minimum value	Use the answer to part a) to rewrite $f(x)$ in terms of $\cos x$ only, then consider the minimum turning point of a cosine graph.	> C
		Min value occurs when $x - \frac{\pi}{4} = \pi \Rightarrow x = \frac{5\pi}{4}$	State value of x at which the minimum occurs **6 marks**		

Paper 2

Question		Answer	Marks	Commentary, hints and tips	Grade demand
1	a)	$f\left(\dfrac{1}{x}-3\right)=\dfrac{1}{\left(\dfrac{1}{x}-3\right)+3}$	Start composite process.	$f(g(x))=\dfrac{1}{g(x)+3}$	C
		$=\dfrac{1}{\dfrac{1}{x}}$	Find $f(g(x))$.		
		$=x$	Express in simplest form.		
	b)	$g(x)=f^{-1}(x)$	State connection.	$f(f^{-1}(x))=x$	
			4 marks		
2		$\overrightarrow{VT}=\overrightarrow{VP}+\overrightarrow{PQ}+\overrightarrow{QT}$	Express $\overrightarrow{VT}$ in terms of $\overrightarrow{VP}$, $\overrightarrow{PQ}$ and $\overrightarrow{PS}$.	Vectors which have the same direction and magnitude are equal, e.g. $\overrightarrow{QT}=\overrightarrow{PS}$.	C
		$=\overrightarrow{VP}+\overrightarrow{PQ}+\dfrac{1}{2}\overrightarrow{PS}$			
		$=\begin{pmatrix}-6\\-11\\-9\end{pmatrix}+\begin{pmatrix}5\\5\\-5\end{pmatrix}+\dfrac{1}{2}\begin{pmatrix}4\\4\\8\end{pmatrix}$	Find components of $\overrightarrow{VP}$, $\overrightarrow{PQ}$ and $\overrightarrow{QT}$.		
		$=\begin{pmatrix}1\\-4\\-10\end{pmatrix}$	Find components of $\overrightarrow{VT}$.		
			3 marks		
3	a)	$A=(2,0)$	Find coordinates of A.	Find the centres of the circles and then use the distance formula.	C
		$B=(10,15)$	Find coordinates of B.		
		$AB=\sqrt{(10-2)^2+(0-15)^2}$	Find distance between centres.		
		$=17$			
	b)	$r_A=\sqrt{(-2)^2+0^2-(-60)}$	Find radius of circle, centre A.	Subtract the sum of the radii from the distance between the centres.	> C
		$=8$			
		$r_B=\sqrt{(-10)^2+(-15)^2-300}$	Find radius of circle, centre B.		
		$=5$			
		gap $=17-(8+5)=4$	Find size of gap.		
			6 marks		

Question		Answer	Marks	Commentary, hints and tips	Grade demand
4	a)	$\overrightarrow{BE} = \dfrac{1}{4}\overrightarrow{BD}$	Interpret ratio.	$DE:EB = 3:1 \Rightarrow \overrightarrow{BE} = \dfrac{1}{4}\overrightarrow{BD}$	C
		$\Rightarrow \mathbf{e} - \mathbf{b} = \dfrac{1}{4}(\mathbf{d} - \mathbf{b})$	Find coordinates of E.		
		$\Rightarrow \mathbf{e} = \dfrac{1}{4}\mathbf{d} + \dfrac{3}{4}\mathbf{b}$			
		$\Rightarrow \mathbf{e} = \begin{pmatrix} 3 \\ 2 \\ 5 \end{pmatrix} + \begin{pmatrix} 18 \\ 12 \\ 0 \end{pmatrix}$			
		$\Rightarrow E(21, 14, 5)$			
	b)	$\overrightarrow{AD} = \begin{pmatrix} -12 \\ 8 \\ 20 \end{pmatrix}$	Find components of $\overrightarrow{AD}$.	$\overrightarrow{AD} = \mathbf{d} - \mathbf{a}$ and $\overrightarrow{AE} = \mathbf{e} - \mathbf{a}$.	C
		$\overrightarrow{AE} = \begin{pmatrix} -3 \\ 14 \\ 5 \end{pmatrix}$	Find components of $\overrightarrow{AE}$.		
	c)	$\overrightarrow{DA}.\overrightarrow{AE} = 248$	Evaluate $\overrightarrow{DA}.\overrightarrow{AE}$	Use vectors that **both** point away from (or towards) the vertex of the angle.	C
		$\|\overrightarrow{DA}\| = \sqrt{608}$ and $\|\overrightarrow{AE}\| = \sqrt{230}$	Evaluate $\|\overrightarrow{DA}\|$ and $\|\overrightarrow{AE}\|$	Don't approximate values of surds, e.g. $\sqrt{608} = 24.7$.	
		$\cos D = \dfrac{248}{\sqrt{608}\sqrt{230}}$	Use scalar product	Premature rounding may lead to an incorrect final answer.	
		angle $DAE = 48.5°$	Calculate angle		
			8 marks		
5	a)	$M_{PQ} = \left(\dfrac{1}{2}, \dfrac{5}{2}\right)$	Calculate midpoint of PQ.	The line is perpendicular to PQ so $m_{\text{line}} \times m_{PQ} = -1$ and it passes through the midpoint of PQ.	C
		$m_{PQ} = 1$	Calculate gradient of PQ.		
		$m_{\text{perp}} = -1$	Calculate gradient of perpendicular.	Since the answer is given, show all the steps from	
		$y - \dfrac{5}{2} = -\left(x - \dfrac{1}{2}\right)$	Demonstrate result.	$y - \dfrac{5}{2} = -\left(x - \dfrac{1}{2}\right)$ to the	
		so $y - \dfrac{5}{2} = -x + \dfrac{1}{2}$		required equation.	
		so $x + y = 3$			
	b)	e.g. $x + y = 3$		The perpendicular bisector of PQ in part (a) and the diameter given in part (b) intersect at the centre of the circle. Use simultaneous equations to find the point of intersection.	C
		$y = 4x - 7$			
		so $x + 4x - 7 = 3$			
		$x = 2$	Find x- (or y- coordinate)		
		$y = 1$	Find y- (or x- coordinate)		
		so $C(2, 1)$			

Question			Answer	Marks	Commentary, hints and tips	Grade demand
5	c)		$r^2 = (3-2)^2 + (5-1)^2 = 17$	Calculate square of radius.		C
			$(x-2)^2 + (y-1)^2 = 17$	State equation of circle.		
				8 marks		
6	a)	(i)	$A_n = 0.04A_{n-1}\ldots$	Start recurrence relation.	Form a recurrence relation which generates a sequence with a limit.	C
			$= 0.04A_{n-1} + 2100$	Complete recurrence relation.		
		(ii)	$L = \dfrac{2100}{1-0.04} = £2187.50$	Find limit.		C
	b)		$2400 = \dfrac{2100}{1-a}$	Substitute into limit formula.	Form an equation involving the limit formula.	C
			$2400(1-a) = 2100$			
			$2400 - 2400a = 2100$			
			$2400a = 300$			
			$a = 0.125$	Find value of a.		
			Rory spend 87.5% of the money in the account each month.	Interpret information and state conclusion.		
				6 marks		
7			$f(x) = \int\left(3 - \dfrac{4}{x^2}\right)dx$	Know to integrate.	Integrate $f'(x)$ to obtain $f(x)$, since integration is the inverse of differentiation.	C
			$= 3x + \dfrac{4}{x} + c$	Integrate.		
			$-1 = 3\times 2 + \dfrac{4}{2} + c$	Substitute for $f(x)$ and x.	Remember to add c, the constant of integration.	
			$\Leftrightarrow -1 = 6 + 2 + c$		Substitute $(2, -1)$ into the result of the integration to find the value of c.	
			$\Rightarrow c = -9$			
			$f(x) = 3x + \dfrac{4}{x} - 9$	Express $f(x)$ in terms of x.		
				4 marks		
8	a)		$243500 \times e^{0.008\times 0} = 243500$	Find population in 2015	In 2015, $t = 0$.	C
	b)		$330000 = 243500e^{0.008t}$	Construct equation.		>C
			$e^{0.008t} = \dfrac{330000}{243500}$	Process equation.	Remember $e^x = y \Leftrightarrow x = \ln y$.	
			$0.008t = \ln\left(\dfrac{3300}{2435}\right)$	Write in logarithmic form.		
			$t = \dfrac{\ln\left(\dfrac{3300}{2435}\right)}{0.008}$	Solve to find number of years.	Don't approximate the value of $\ln\left(\dfrac{3300}{2435}\right)$. Premature rounding may lead to an incorrect final answer.	
			$= 38$ years			
				5 marks		

Question	Answer	Marks	Commentary, hints and tips	Grade demand
9	$b^2 - 4ac = (1-k)^2 - 4(1-k)$ $= k^2 + 2k - 3$ $= (k-1)(k+3)$ Roots are 1 and -3 $(k-1)(k+3) > 0$ $k < -3, k > 1$ with eg table of signs or sketch	Use the discriminant Identify roots of quadratic expression Apply $b^2 - 4ac > 0$ State range with justification	Two real and distinct roots so $b^2 - 4ac > 0$. Use a table of values or a sketch graph of $y = (k-1)(k+3)$ to solve $(k-1)(k+3) > 0$. 	> C

Table for question 9:

k	$\rightarrow$	-3	$\rightarrow$	1	$\rightarrow$
$k^2 + 2k - 3$	$+$	0	$-$	0	$+$

4 marks

Question	Answer	Marks	Commentary, hints and tips	Grade demand
10	$f'(x) = 3x^2 \ldots$ $3x^2 + 2x - 5 = 0$ $(3x+5)(x-1) = 0$ $x = -\dfrac{5}{3}, x = 1$	Know to and differentiate one term Complete differentiation and equate to zero Factorise derivative Solve for x	The stationary points occur at points where $f'(x) = 0$.	C

4 marks

Question	Answer	Marks	Commentary, hints and tips	Grade demand
11	**Method 1** $\log_e y = \log_e be^{ax}$ $\log_e y = \log_e b + \log_e e^{ax}$ $\log_e y = ax + \log_e b$ $a = \dfrac{4.5}{3} = 1.5$ $\log_e b = 4.5$ $\Rightarrow b = e^{4.5} = 90$ **Method 2** $\log_e y = 1.5x + 4.5$ $y = e^{1.5x + 4.5}$ $y = e^{1.5x} \times e^{4.5}$ $y = 90e^{1.5x}$ $a = 1.5, b = 90$	**Method 1** Take logs of both sides of equation. Use $\log_e xy = \log_e x + \log_e y$ and $\log_e e^{ax} = ax \log_e e = ax$. Find a. Find b. **Method 2** State linear equation. Convert to exponential form. Use law of indices. Obtain result.	Use laws of logarithms to rearrange $y = be^{ax}$ into the form $\log_e y = ax + \log_e b$. This is the equation of the straight line with gradient a and y-intercept $(0, \log_e b)$. Remember $\log_e b = y \Leftrightarrow b = e^y$. The straight line has equation $\log_e y = mx + c$. Use laws of logarithms to rearrange this equation into the form $y = be^{ax}$. Remember $\log_e y = x \Leftrightarrow y = e^x$.	> C

4 marks

Question		Answer	Marks	Commentary, hints and tips	Grade demand
12	a)	$a = v'(t)$ $= 5 - 2t$	Know to differentiate. Differentiate.	Acceleration is the rate of change of velocity with respect to time, i.e. $a = v\cdot(t)$.	> C
	b)	$s(t) = \int v(t)\,dt$ $= t + \dfrac{5}{2}t^2 - \dfrac{1}{3}t^3 + c$ $s(0) = 2 \Rightarrow c = 2$ $\Rightarrow s(t) = t + \dfrac{5}{2}t^2 - \dfrac{1}{3}t^3 + 2$ **5 marks**	Know to integrate. Integrate. Determine constant and state $s(t)$.	Velocity is the rate of change of displacement with respect to time, i.e. $v = s\cdot(t)$ so $s = \int v(t)\,dt$. Remember to add c, the constant of integration. Substitute $s = 2$ and $t = 0$ into the result of the integration to find the value of c.	> C
13		$2\cos^2\theta - 1 + \cos\theta = 0$ $2\cos^2\theta + \cos\theta - 1 = 0$ $(2\cos\theta - 1)(\cos\theta + 1) = 0$ $\cos\theta = \dfrac{1}{2}, \cos\theta = -1$ $\theta = \dfrac{\pi}{3}, \dfrac{5\pi}{3}, \pi$ **4 marks**	Use double angle formula. Rearrange and factorise. Solve for $\cos\theta$. Solve for θ.	Use the substitution $\cos 2\theta = 2\cos^2\theta - 1$ to obtain an equation with terms in $\cos\theta$ only. Use exact values to give the answers in terms of π.	> C